THE MONETARY AND FINANCIAL SYSTEM

second edition

Peter Dunkley
Peter Gutmann

Osborne Books

First edition 1990

Published and typeset by
Osborne Books Limited, Gwernant,
The Common,
Lower Broadheath, Worcester WR2 6RP.

Printed by The Bath Press, Avon.

British Library Cataloguing-in-Publication Data: a catalogue record for this book is available from the British Library.

ISBN 1-872962-45-9

introduction

This book has been designed primarily as a convenient and comprehensive revision aid for students studying for The Monetary and Financial System examination. Teachers of the subject will also find the book useful. Its focus on all the key areas of the syllabus will help ensure complete coverage without burdening students with unnecessary detail.

Experience in answering questions is very important for examination success. A particularly useful feature of the contents of this book is the selection of questions set in recent years. Some guidance - in the form of references to relevant parts of the text and short notes - is provided to help the student construct the appropriate answer. Further relevant details for inclusion in the answer should, of course, be extracted from the recommended text books.

Peter Dunkley
Peter Gutmann

acknowledgements

Thanks are due to Jean Cox, Carolyn Hughes and George Johnston for help with the production of the text, and to The Chartered Institute of Bankers and the Bank of England for permission to quote from published sources.

the authors

Peter Dunkley is Director of Risk and Capital in National Westminster Bank's Group Treasury and Capital Markets. He has for a long time been involved in the teaching of this subject, and is Moderator for correspondence courses.

Peter Gutmann is Senior Research Manager in National Westminster Bank's economics department. He has been involved in this subject for many years, initially as a teacher, and from 1984 to 1991 as Chief Examiner.

contents

Unit 1	**Money and Inflation**	
1.1	The functions of money	1
1.2	Liquidity and near-money	1
1.3	The monetary aggregates	3
1.4	Monetary targets	4
1.5	Money and inflation	4
1.6	Changes in the value of money	7
Unit 2	**Financial Institutions**	
2.1	Financial intermediation	10
2.2	The commercial banks	13
2.3	Bank liquidity	16
2.4	The Bank of England	18
2.5	The building societies	20
2.6	Other financial intermediaries	21
Unit 3	**Financial Markets in the UK**	
3.1	The role of the Bank of England	25
3.2	The London money markets	27
3.3	The eurocurrency markets	31
3.4	The capital markets	33
Unit 4	**The Money Supply**	
4.1	Lending to the private sector	37
4.2	The fiscal balance	39
4.3	Funding the PSBR	41
4.4	Overseas influences	42
4.5	Money supply changes: summary	42
4.6	Introduction to techniques for controlling the money supply	44
4.7	Changes in the money supply and bank balance sheets	44

Unit 5	**Interest Rates**	
5.1	Real and nominal interest rates	47
5.2	Factors affecting interest rates	48
5.3	The yield curve	51
5.4	Effects of a change in interest rates	52
5.5	Domestic interest rates, eurocurrency rates and exchange rates	54
Unit 6	**Economic Policy**	
6.1	Aims and objectives	58
6.2	Monetary policy	59
6.3	Fiscal policy	64
6.4	Prices and incomes policy	65
6.5	Exchange rate policy	65
6.6	The effectiveness of economic policy	66
Unit 7	**The Balance of Payments**	
7.1	Structure of balance of payments	69
7.2	The current account	71
7.3	The capital account	72
7.4	Current account deficits	73
Unit 8	**Exchange Rates**	
8.1	Operation of the market	79
8.2	Factors affecting exchange rates	80
8.3	Exchange rate systems	81
8.4	Floating and fixed: which is better ?	83
8.5	Trade-weighted (effective) rates	84
8.6	The European Monetary System (EMS)	85
8.7	Exchange rates and interest rates	88
Unit 9	**Supervision and Regulation**	
9.1	The role of the Bank of England	91
9.2	European Community (EC) regulations	93
9.3	The Third World debt problem	94
9.4	Investment business	95
9.5	Building societies	96
9.6	Insurance companies	96
Unit 10	**Corporate Finance and Risk Management**	
10.1	Short-term finance	98
10.2	Medium/long-term finance	99
10.3	Equity finance	101
10.4	Rate risk management	101
10.5	Exchange rate risk	103

Unit One
Money and Inflation

1.1 The functions of money

Money can be defined as anything which is generally acceptable in exchange for goods and services and is a necessary part of any developed society. Its contribution to economic efficiency stems from its functions as:

A medium of exchange
Money facilitates exchange and overcomes the basic problems of barter, notably the need for a 'double coincidence of wants'. Money thus makes possible the division of labour and specialisation.

A measure of value or unit of account
Money serves as a unit in which the differing value of widely diverse commodities or services can be expressed with precision.

A store of wealth
Many commodities depreciate as time passes, or may be impractical to store. Money is used to store wealth, although in times of rapid inflation people look for other methods.

A standard for deferred payments
If credit is to be made available, there must be some generally acceptable method by which debts may be denominated, assessed and understood.

1.2 Liquidity and near-money

❑ Liquidity

The general acceptability of money - a vital attribute - makes it the most *liquid* of assets. *Liquidity* means that:

- an asset is immediately and always exchangeable in full payment for goods and services
- there is no loss of capital or significant interest in turning the asset into cash.

Money itself is, by definition, completely liquid. At the other end of the *'liquidity spectrum'* are non-financial assets such as land. The holder of such an asset will have to pay marketing costs and may have to wait some time until a buyer emerges, if he wishes to realise it.

❑ Near-money

Nearer the liquid end of the spectrum are certain financial assets which are defined as *'near-money'* or *'quasi-money'* because though not as liquid as cash or current accounts, such assets can be realised rapidly and with little or no loss. Examples are: certificates of deposit and Treasury bills. Financial innovations have made some interest-bearing deposits much more liquid. Most are available on demand or at very short notice and are now often used for transactions purposes.

The close substitutability and lack of obvious dividing lines between deposits with banks and with building societies has led to some problems in defining monetary aggregates. The distinction between banks and building societies has become blurred, and this has led to changes in definitions of the money supply.

❑ 'Narrow' and 'broad money'

'Narrow' measures of the money stock are *transaction* based, comprising assets which may be instantly used as a means of payment - notes and coin, current accounts, and easy access bank deposit and building society accounts. Such measures focus on money's function as a means of exchange.

'Broad' measures comprise the above plus more *savings - oriented* assets which can quickly and without loss be turned into cash - such as wholesale deposits and money market instruments. Such measures focus on money's function as a means of exchange *and* a store of wealth.

1.3 The monetary aggregates

The range of money supply definitions used in the UK has been rationalised in recent years in recognition of the fact that for monetary control purposes:

- it is no longer meaningful to differentiate between interest-bearing and non-interest-bearing deposits
- the close similarity between bank and building society deposits means that they may be treated as the same product

The measures currently used in the UK are:

MO *The narrowest definition comprising:*

- notes and coin in circulation with the public
- banks' till money
- banks' operational deposits with the Bank of England

M2 *A narrow measure consisting of all sterling deposits used for transactions purposes :*

- notes and coin in circulation with the public
- retail bank deposits (ie deposits of less than £100,000)
- retail building society shares and deposits
- National Savings Bank ordinary accounts

M4 *A broad definition comprising:*

- notes and coin in circulation with the public
- all bank deposits
- all building society shares and deposits
- bank and building society CDs

❑ Why are there several definitions?

- There is a need to consider different aspects of money such as transactions and savings.
- There are many liquid assets in a modern economy - so no one definition provides an accurate guide.
- Changes occurring in the financial environment, for example the blurring of distinctions between banks and building societies.

1.4 Monetary targets

Publicly announced targets for money supply growth are often set by the authorities in modern economies for the following reasons:

- as a guide to official policy
- to inform the public that the authorities intend to control the money supply and inflation, and this resolve would help dampen expectations about future inflation

During the 1980s in the UK, money supply measures such as M2 and M4 rose strongly - at around 18% per annum in the case of M4 - partly due to innovation and liberalisation in the financial markets. Changes in the regulatory environment contributed to a rapid rise in consumer credit. The authorities ceased to target the M2 and M4 measures since it became difficult to interpret their behaviour in these changing circumstances.

A target for MO is still set, and since 1987 this has been the only targeted measure (although the behaviour of the other definitions is closely monitored). However, MO, which consists largely of notes and coins in circulation, has little credibility as a pointer to future developments.

Problems in interpreting the behaviour of monetary growth led to disillusionment in the late 1980s with an approach which focused on the connection between money supply changes and other economic variables. However, an appreciation of the economic implications of monetary growth is still relevant, and the following section shows a theoretical justification for this in relation to inflation.

1.5 Money and inflation

❑ The quantity theory of money

The basic idea behind the quantity theory is that there is a close link between the amount of money in the economy, and the level of prices. In order to demonstrate the link clearly, the following equation was developed, often known as 'Fisher's formula':

MV = PT

where

M = the quantity of money in the economy.
V = velocity of circulation - this is the speed at which money moves through the economy in any given period. An increase in velocity implies an increase in spending, and has a similar effect to an increase in money stock.
P = the level of prices.
T = the number of transactions in a given time period.

Critics emphasise that:

- the formula is a tautology - the statement must be true because MV equals total expenditure and PT total sales; therefore it is not helpful in linking money supply and prices.

- the formula only works in explaining the link between M and P if V and T are held to be constant.

- there is no generally accepted definition of M.

Modern monetarists acknowledge the limitations of the Fisher formula, but still argue that there is a close and direct relationship between the money supply and the rate of inflation. If monetary policy accommodates cost pressures (such as demands for higher wages, or higher profits - i.e. *cost-push* inflation) then consumer prices will rise.

Inflation may also be attributed to *demand-pull* where demand is rising more rapidly than supply, causing prices to rise.

❑ Effects of inflation on money's functions

Inflation can have an unfavourable impact on the functions of money. Which of the functions is affected will depend on how rapid the rate of inflation is.

❑ The first to be affected is money's function as a *store of value* so that people begin to look to other ways of preserving their wealth by investing in non-financial assets.

❑ Money as a *unit of account* is also affected quite early in a situation of accelerating inflation. Accounting techniques have to be amended in order to make meaningful comparisons over time. At very rapid inflation rates (hyper-inflation) the unit may be revalued to reduce the size of figures people have to cope with in monetary transactions.

❑ The other functions of money would also be affected by hyper-inflation. Forward *calculation of debts* would become meaningless because the rate of interest demanded would have to be enormous in order to justify a loan. Eventually, as confidence in the money unit evaporated, other commodities would be used as a *medium of exchange.*

❑ Index-linking

The index-linking of financial assets is a method which has been used in the UK and other countries to cope with periods of high inflation. Such a system ensures that a sum of money (e.g. a salary, a deposit in the bank) has the same purchasing power at the end of a given period as at the beginning, despite inflation. This is done by linking the capital value of the asset to the rise in prices as expressed by an index of retail prices (see section 1.6).

Assets which have been index-linked in the UK include:

- some National Savings certificates
- some gilt-edged stock
- some savings through SAYE schemes operated by the Department for National Savings

Civil servants' pensions are also index-linked. In some other countries where inflation is much higher than in the UK, financial transactions such as wages and salaries and debts are index-linked, while ensuring that the interests of employees, lenders, etc. are protected. It is important to realise that such a scheme only attacks the symptoms of inflation, not the root causes.

1.6 Measurement of changes in the value of money

Changes in money's own value (e.g. inflation where the value of money is falling) can only be calculated in terms of the things (goods and services) against which money exchanges. Attempts are made to measure changes in the value of money over a period by reference to a basket of goods which a given amount of money can buy at the beginning and end of the period under review.

❑ The Retail Price Index (RPI)

The best known method of measuring such changes is the index number method, expressed in the UK by the general *index of retail prices* (the RPI) series. This index registers the prices of a collection of goods and services entering a typical 'shopping basket', the prices of the commodities recorded being weighted to reflect their relative importance in the public's household budget. By altering the weights, changes in spending habits can be reflected in the index. For example, the weight accorded to food decreased from 19% in 1974 to 15% in 1989. There is clearly some distortion of the index in this process but it overcomes to some extent difficulties of coping with changes in spending patterns over a longer period.

❑ Further indicators

The retail price index is only one of several indicators of inflation. A similar index is monitored for producer (whosesale) prices and there is also a 'deflator' for gross domestic product as a whole (*the GDP deflator).* This is obtained by dividing estimated current prices of all goods and services which make up national income by the corresponding estimate at constant prices.

Inflation in the UK is often measured these days by reference to the "underlying" rate of inflation, which excludes from the RPI the impact of mortgage interest payments, following the practice in much of the rest of Europe.

questions and answers

Q 1 (a) What is meant by index-linking of financial assets? Include some examples of index-linked assets in your answer. (9)

(b) To what extent is index-linking likely to succeed in curbing inflation? How else might governments attempt to deal with the problem? (16)

(Spring 1986)

Answer

(a) See section 1.5

(b) Index-linking attacks only the symptoms of inflation. Monetary policy, prices and incomes controls, and fiscal policy need to be directed at the root causes of inflation to deal with the problem.

Q 2 (a) Distinguish between narrow and broad concepts of the money stock, briefly illustrating your answer with reference to the definitions used in any country with which you are familiar. (13)

(b) Indicate, giving reasons, whether the following are included in measures of money, and in each case state whether it is the broad or narrow measure:
(i) certificates of deposit issued by banks;
(ii) building society term shares;
(iii) bank current accounts;
(iv) equity shares in a public company. (12).

(Autumn1987)

Answer

(a) See section 1.2

(b) See section 1.3

(i) Broad only

(ii) Broad only - no transactions element

(iii) Narrow and broad - held primarily for transactions

(iv) Not included- these are not liquid assets, liable to capital loss.

Q3 (a) Why is it considered necessary to have more than one definition of the money supply? (7)

(b) Why is it considered necessary to monitor and target money supply growth? (10)

(c) State whether the following are included in measures of money. In each case, indicate whether it is in the broad or narrow measure and give reasons for its appearance in, or exclusion from, the money supply:
(i) treasury bills
(ii) equity shares in a company
(iii) gilt-edged securities. (8)

(adapted from Spring 1990)

Answer
(a) See section 1.3
(b) See sections 1.4 and 1.5
(c) See section 1.3

Q4 (a) How do the authorities of a country measure the rate of inflation? (8)
(b) Describe the relationship between the money supply and the rate of inflation. (5)
(c) What problems are caused by inflation? (12)

(Autumn 1991)

Answer
(a) See section 1.6
(b) See section 1.5
(c) See section 1.5; also exports became uncompetitive, causing balance of payments problems; there is an arbitrary redistribution of income, with those on fixed incomes losing out. With hyper-inflation there is great economic uncertainty and a breakdown of the price mechanism.

Q5 (a) Describe briefly the four main functions of money. (8)
(b) To what extent is each function affected by inflation, and how in each case can the problems which arise be overcome? (17)

(Spring 1992)

Answer
(a) See section 1.1
(b) See section 1.5

Unit Two
UK Financial Institutions

2.1 Financial intermediation

Financial intermediaries exist to transfer funds from one sector of the economy to another, e.g. from the personal sector to the corporate sector.

This may involve simply the transformation of a bank deposit into a bank loan, i.e. within the same institution.

Alternatively, intermediation may reflect the movement of funds from one type of institution such as a building society to a 'non-deposit-taking' institution, such as an insurance company or a pension fund.

In broad terms, then, financial intermediation involves the channelling of funds from those sectors which have a financial surplus (usually but not always the personal sector) to those sectors which have a deficit. The table below illustrates this situation:

Flow of funds matrix (1991 2nd quarter)

	Surplus (+) Deficit (-) £M
Public sector	- 4,732
Financial institutions	- 1,583
Industrial and commercial companies	- 1,528
Personal sector	+ 8,182
Overseas sector	+ 1,031
Residual error	- 1,370

Source: Bank of England Quarterly Bulletin

There are essentially two types of financial intermediary: deposit-taking institutions and non-deposit-taking institutions. As intermediaries they are involved in:

- *Risk transformation* - the diversification of a depositor's risk by lending his funds to a wide variety of borrowers.

- *Maturity transformation* - the employment of short-term deposits at, say, seven days notice or less, into a five year loan. This satisfies the lender's wish for liquidity, and the borrower's desire to have long-term finance.

- *Aggregation* - the channelling of numerous small deposits (or premiums in the case of life assurance companies) as well as large deposits taken from corporate customers or direct from the money market, into a wide variety of loans and investments, again both large and small. The financial intermediary provides the conduit through which the funds flow in both directions.

❑ Disintermediation

This development was specifically associated with the deregulation and globalisation of financial services in many advanced countries. Disintermediation effectively means that borrowers and lenders (investors) are put into direct contact with each other and the bank or financial institution merely acts as a broker or underwriter for the transaction:

- *Commercial paper*, which was first introduced in the UK in 1986, is an obvious example whereby industrial and commercial companies issue short term securities direct to investors.

- Disintermediation is also associated with *securitisation* whereby traditional bank lending is replaced by tradeable securities, such as bonds. In the US securitisation is well developed and covers mortgages as well as consumer receivables and credit cards.

❑ Deposit-taking institutions

These are most obviously represented by the clearing banks, savings banks, building societies and finance houses. All of these are heavily reliant on the personal sector as a source of funds, although 'wholesale' deposits raised in the inter-bank market are now important.

❑ Non-deposit-taking institutions

These include life assurance companies, pension funds, unit trusts and investment trusts. A common feature is that 'small' investors can invest regularly, usually on a contractual basis, to provide a future source of income.

Risk transformation is achieved by investing these savings in a portfolio of assets to earn interest or achieve capital gain, usually in the form of company securities (equities) or government gilt-edged stock. The assets of such institutions are mainly long-term in nature, achieving the maturity transformation which is a feature of financial intermediaries in general.

❑ Wholesale and retail funds

Retail deposits are traditionally associated with UK banking as operated through the clearing bank domestic branch system, e.g. current accounts, seven day notice deposit accounts and higher interest accounts. Building societies also collect retail deposits, essentially from the personal sector.

Banks and building societies raise much of their funding from the *wholesale money markets* in the form of inter-bank deposits at LIBID(London Inter-bank bid rate) or through the issue of Certificates of Deposit (CDs).

The concept of a wholesale deposit is inevitably vague and there is no formal definition. Generally, wholesale deposits are for large amounts, and are collected via the inter-bank market or through the issue of CDs, from personal and corporate investors, as well as other financial institutions. Wholesale funds attract higher rates of interest than retail deposits.

On the lending side, bank advances linked to base rate are usually referred to as 'retail' loans, whilst advances priced against LIBOR (London Inter-Bank Offered Rate) would be wholesale or market lending.

2.2 The commercial banks

There are well over 400 banks in the UK recognised by the Bank of England. These include the retail banks, merchant banks, other British banks, American, Japanese and other overseas banks. The discount market is treated separately for statistical purposes.

❑ Retail banks

These include the London and Scottish Clearing Banks, Northern Ireland banks, Girobank and Abbey National PLC. Retail banks are associated with large branch networks, a wide and varied customer base with a large personal element and the clearing, (i.e. the exchange and settlement) of cheques. Their basic functions are as follows:

- **To provide the country's main payments mechanism** through the Bankers Clearing House and Bank Giro. The Clearing House Automated Payments System (CHAPS) allows for same-day transaction of funds in large amounts anywhere in the UK.

- **The provision of credit**, by way of overdraft, fixed term loan, medium term lending schemes and home mortgages. Credit cards (eg Mastercard and Visa) fund a substantial amount of consumer spending, while finance for hire purchase and leasing is provided through the banks' various finance house subsidiaries.

- **Other services** such as standing orders, direct debits, executor and trustee work, taxation advice and foreign exchange are traditional. More recent services include merchant banking (via subsidiaries), factoring, insurance broking, payroll services and unit trusts. The provision of services through automated teller machines (ATMs) is now very widespread and includes building societies as well as banks. The banks also provide a variety of cash management schemes for the corporate sector.

❑ The banks' balance sheet

The figures below – taken from the Bank of England Quarterly Bulletin – highlight the main sources of funds for such banks and the use to which those funds are put to earn profit.

Banks in the UK: balance sheet March 1992

Source: Bank of England Quarterly Bulletin

LIABILITIES	£bn	£bn
Sterling deposits		
UK banks	84.7	
UK private sector	299.6	
UK public sector	6.0	
Overseas residents	72.1	
Certificates of deposit	50.7	
		513.1
Foreign currency deposits		618.3
Other liabilities (mainly capital)		114.6
		1,246.0
ASSETS		
Sterling:		
Cash and balances with the Bank of England		4.3
Market loans:		
Discount houses	8.9	
Other UK banks	78.9	
Certificates of deposit held	21.7	
Local Authorities	0.6	
Overseas	23.8	
		133.9
Treasury and other bills		13.6
British government and other stocks		31.6
Advances		379.7
Foreign currency assets		648.0
Other assets		34.9
Total assets		1,246.0

Notes on the banks' balance sheet:

Liabilities

On the *liabilities* side, it can be seen that for sterling deposits the UK private sector (i.e. people and companies) is the largest provider of funds. These funds comprise current accounts, deposit accounts and higher interest accounts, both personal and corporate. Deposits from the UK banks, and the issue of certificates of deposit (CDs) reflect inter-bank transactions and the use of 'wholesale' or money market deposits as a funding source.

Currency deposits represent around one fifth of UK retail banks' liabilities, but this proportion is, of course, considerably higher for American, Japanese and other overseas banks, as can be seen from the table opposite, which covers all banks in the UK.

Assets

Sterling *assets* include the Bank of England cash ratio deposits and market loans to other UK banks, as well as to the discount market (LDMA), and holdings of other banks' CD's. Holdings of bills of exchange and investments in short-term government stocks have importance for liquidity purposes. Advances to the UK private sector is the largest single item and includes retail overdrafts linked to base rate as well as personal loans, fixed rate loans to the corporate sector, LIBOR-based lending and mortgage loans.

Currency assets are mainly in the form of market loans and advances and broadly match currency liabilities.

Off-balance sheet items

The published balance sheet does not, however, give a complete picture of the business of a modern commercial bank. Off-balance sheet items, such as foreign exchange and interest rate swaps can be very significant and for many banks, this business is a major source of income.

❑ British merchant banks (investment banks)

This group comprises those UK banks which are members of the British Merchant Banks and Securities Houses Association. They are involved in corporate finance; investment management; foreign exchange and gold dealing; financial advice including capital reorganisation, mergers and acquisitions, dividend policy; capital issues including eurobonds; commercial paper, etc.

The late 1980s saw a massive reorganisation of the merchant bank sector and there are few independent organisations still in existence. Most investment banks are now part of larger banking groups owned by the major UK clearing banks as well as banks from abroad.

❑ Foreign banks

London has hundreds of foreign banks of all sizes, most of which are situated in the City of London. Banks from the US and Japan are the most numerous, but all of the world's major banks are represented.

Representation can take the form of a branch, subsidiary or simply a representative office. One of the changes associated with Big Bang in the late 1980s was the take-over of a number of stockbrokers, jobbers and financial services companies by foreign banks.

The business of foreign banks traditionally was in eurocurrency, trade finance and foreign exchange. Foreign banks now have both direct and indirect involvement in merchant banking activities, securities business and even in mortgage finance.

2.3 Bank liquidity

From experience, banks have learnt that a certain ratio between cash and total deposits is necessary in order to provide cover to ensure they will not be faced with a liquidity problem. This ratio will, of course, vary between different banks according to the nature of their business and the type of depositor. In some countries, there are rigid guidelines on the types and amounts of liquid assets which banks must hold. In the UK the Bank of England defines certain assets which should be included, but is more flexible on the actual 'liquidity' ratio itself.

Liquid assets include cash and Bank of England working balances; secured money at call with 'reputable' institutions such as discount houses and certain money brokers, Gilt-Edged Market Makers (GEMMs) and Stock Exchange money brokers. Also included are Treasury bills, and eligible bank bills as well as short-dated gilt-edged government stocks.

A bank requires liquidity

- to meet the withdrawal of deposits
- to settle the clearing
- to provide for unexpected demands for cash
- to maintain confidence

Any bank's policy for liquidity has two main aspects: firstly, how much liquidity the bank itself requires in relation to its own business, and secondly, whether the authorities decide how much liquidity is required for regulatory purposes, i.e. 'system' liquidity.

Apart from their holdings of short-term realisable assets, banks must take account of other factors in formulating their own liquidity strategy:

- The extent to which the bank has a diversified deposit base. In general terms, a 'retail' bank has more direct customers than a wholesale bank, which relies on large single deposits (including CDs) from a relatively small number of investors.

- The ability to raise deposits, when necessary, from the inter-bank market. This depends upon confidence in the bank and also the country in which the bank operates.

- The cash flow generated from maturing assets. A bank must ensure that the maturity profiles of its loans and deposits are mutually acceptable and that an adequate proportion of its advances is maturing to meet any likely net repayment of deposits.

- Liquidity strategy is closely associated with asset and liability management, which has become an essential part of any modern bank's day-to-day activities. Banks are concerned to limit the risks inherent in the maturity mismatches between their deposits and their loans. Interest rate swaps are often used to reduce risk.

The most profitable of any bank's assets tend to be the least liquid, i.e. advances and investments. The banker's dilemma is this: to maximise profitability by keeping these remunerative assets at a high level, whilst at the same time safeguarding the liquidity position by keeping adequate but less profitable liquid assets to repay depositors on demand. A compromise between the desire for profits and the need for liquidity is essential.

2.4 The Bank of England

The Bank of England is the central bank for the UK, founded in 1694 and nationalised in 1946. The Bank is an agent of government. It provides advice and analysis on economic policy and implements monetary policy. Its activities are greatly influenced by the Banking Acts, the most recent being the Banking Act 1987.

The Bank's role in the UK is very similar to that carried out by most central banks around the world in relation to their own economies.

❑ Functions of the Bank of England

The issue of notes
This has been a monopoly of the Bank in England and Wales since the Bank Charter Act of 1844. In Scotland, Northern Ireland and the Isle of Man, certain banks continue to issue notes.

Banker to the government

- Accounts are maintained for the Exchequer and other government departments. The Bank acts as registrar for the public debt and advises the government on any new issues or conversions, carrying out the necessary administrative work.

- The Bank operates the Central Gilts Office (CGO) through which pass all dealings in government securities carried out by the Gilt Edged Market Makers (GEMMs) and the commercial banks.

- The Bank operates the Exchange Equalization Account which holds the country's convertible currency reserves and through which it can intervene in the foreign exchange markets to influence sterling's external value.

Banker to the commercial banks

The Bank of England acts for the commercial banks in much the same way that any bank acts for its customers. Clearing differences are settled through central bank accounts and the commercial banks must therefore hold sufficient 'operational' balances at the Bank to cover such settlements.

Lender of last resort

The Bank of England is the ultimate supporter of the banking system and ensures that the 'system' always balances.

Large transactions between government departments and the private sector, (e.g. payment of corporation tax, sales of gilt-edged stock) result in substantial net flows of money between the Bank of England and the commercial banks. This results in temporary surpluses and shortages. Through its operations in the money markets (see Unit 3) which are often carried out via the discount houses, the Bank is able to offset these flows, while at the same time influencing the general direction of interest rates by varying the terms on which support is provided or excess funds removed from the system.

These day-to-day activities, which can involve the buying and selling of commercial bills of exchange, Treasury bills, short-term government securities, local authority bonds, ECGD loans and repurchase agreements (REPOs) may be viewed collectively as *open market* operations.

Debt management

As banker to the government, the Bank of England is responsible for ensuring that its borrowing needs are met. These comprise government long-term borrowing in the form of gilt-edged stock and the residual short-term borrowing in the form of Treasury bills.

Treasury bills are usually issued for 91 days and are sold at a discount, generally by tender. The minimum denomination is £50,000. The treasury bill issue can be used by the authorities to influence the level of short-term interest rates, and the total weekly tender may be raised or lowered to take account of the flows of money into and out of the short-term markets. The Bank of England buys and sells Treasury bills and eligible bank bills as part of its day-to-day operations in the money markets.

Implementation of monetary policy

- By open market operations
- By influencing short-term interest rates
- By issuing directives to, or by applying informal pressure on, the banking system, for example in relation to the volume or type of lending that may be undertaken.
- By imposing balance sheet constraints (e.g. special deposits) directly or by implication. Capital adequacy requirements also effectively limit balance sheet growth.

Research

In its role as adviser to the government, the Bank undertakes a great deal of research into the economy in general and the financial sector in particular. Various academic articles are published in the Bank's Quarterly Bulletin.

Supervisory and regulatory roles

These roles are included in Unit 9, but should not be excluded from any general discussion of the Bank's functions

2.5 The building societies

Building societies represent a major force in the personal savings market as well as in their traditional role as providers of mortgage finance. Their activities have expanded rapidly in recent years and some of the larger societies are almost indistinguishable from banks in terms of the services they provide.

The most significant development in the history of the building society movement was the Building Societies Act 1986 which came into effect on 1 January 1987. The main provisions of the Act are as follows:

- The *principal* purpose of building societies remains that of raising funds from their members, for making advances to members for their residential use.
- The Act allows societies to engage in other forms of lending, secured and unsecured, within strict limits. For example, "Class 3" commercial assets which include loans for mobile homes, unsecured loans, investment properties, etc., must not exceed 5% of total assets.
- On the funding side, in order to retain the characteristics of a mutual building society, non-retail funds and deposits are not to exceed 40% of the society's total liabilities.
- The Act sets out criteria for prudent management which includes capital adequacy requirements and controls on liquidity.
- Whilst the larger societies now have a much greater degree of flexibility in the services they offer, *all* societies can provide certain services including money transmission, foreign exchange to individuals, insurance advice, conveyancing, administration of pension schemes, etc.

Clearly the line between what is a building society and what is a bank is extremely thin and one society - the Abbey National - opted to become a fully public limited company operating within the banking sector.

2.6 Other financial intermediaries

❑ National Savings Bank

National Savings Bank (NSB) is a public corporation which was created in 1969 and is operated through the Post Office branch network. It issues National Savings Certificates, runs "Save As You Earn" schemes and provides bank accounts, both ordinary accounts and investment accounts. NSB savings contribute to funding of the Public Sector Borrowing Requirement.

❑ Finance houses

Finance houses were originally associated with the provision of hire purchase and leasing finance to private individuals and the corporate sector. They are often subsidiaries of the larger UK commercial banks and provide a wide variety of services from deposit accounts through to personal loans and factoring facilities for small and medium sized businesses. Funding (i.e deposits) is obtained both from individuals and from companies, and finance houses are also very active in the short-term money markets. They are, in effect, involved in both retail and wholesale banking activities. For statistical purposes Finance houses appear in the "Other British Banks" table of the Bank of England Quarterly Bulletin.

❑ Insurance companies and pension funds

Insurance companies and pension funds are an important element of the UK financial system. They compete with the banks for the savings of the personal sector, but must, of necessity, take a much longer view of their potential financial commitments for policy-holders and future recipients of pensions. Both types of institution invest in government securities (gilts), and also in company securities (equities or long-dated bonds). A number of the major UK banks now have insurance subsidiaries, and - through their merchant banking links - manage large investment portfolios and pension funds.

❑ Investment trusts and unit trusts

Investment trusts and unit trusts can be regarded as savings institutions whose purpose is to spread risk by investing in a wide range of securities.

Investment trusts are limited companies who issue shares. Their assets comprise mainly equities, but can include shorter term investments such as bank Certificates of Deposit and short-term gilts. Investment trusts appeal to those looking for a longer term investment with a higher degree of risk (and thus potential reward) than is provided by, say, a building society deposit or a long-dated government stock.

Unit trusts have some features in common with investment trusts in that their funds are invested in a variety of assets, mainly equities. The unit trust company manages the investment of its funds, which are obtained by issuing units. These units can be sold back to the trust at any time and their "price" will reflect the current market valuation of all the the investments into which the trust has placed its money.

questions and answers

Q 1 (a) What does the concept of liquidity mean in relation to (i) an individual, (ii) a commercial bank?
(b) How do commercial banks provide for liquidity?

(Spring 1986)

Answer

(a) See sections 1.2 and 2.3
(b) See sections 2.2 and 2.3

Q 2 Is it essential for a country to have a central bank?

(Autumn 1986)

Answer

See section 2.4 and Unit 9 for the functions carried out by a typical central bank. These functions are vital, but they do not have to be performed by a central bank. Other agencies such as commercial banks could act as banker to the government, for example. However, the lender of last resort function is best carried out by a central bank.

Q 3 (a) What are the basic benefits arising from financial intermediation? (10)
(b) What do you understand by the term 'disintermediation'? (5)
(c) Outline the clearing banks' response to:
(i) challenges from the building societies in the area of financial intermediation;
(ii) challenges from developments in the UK capital markets in the area of disintermediation. (10)

(Spring 1987)

Answer

(a) See section 2.1

(b) See section 2.1

(c) (i) Banks have introduced a variety of deposit account schemes and have taken the building societies on in the mortage market. They are advertising and marketing more aggressively; some branches open on Saturdays.

(ii) Banks have acquired stock-brokers, jobbers, and merchant banks. They offer a share-dealing service in large branches.

Q 4 Outline the ways in which the Bank of England carries out its role as:

(a) banker to the government;

(b) banker to the banks;

(c) lender of the last resort to the banking system

(Autumn 1988)

Answer

See section 2.4

Q 5 What are the advantages and disadvantages to building societies of converting to plc status?

(Spring 1992)

Answer

See section 2.5. The major advantage is freedom from the restrictions imposed by the Building Societies Act 1986, eg

- *limits on unsecured lending (maximum 15% of assets)*
- *limits on lending to the corporate sector*
- *limits on capital raising, eg by rights issue (although they can now issue Permanent Interest Bearing Shares [PIBS])*
- *expansion is by merger with other societies or internal growth – takeovers of other financial institutions is not encouraged*

Disadvantages in converting to plc status include:

- *Bank of England supervision could be more onerous and would involve high costs in adapting to a new set of requirements and statistical returns*
- *pressure to pay dividends may reduce retained earnings*
- *institutional investors may exercise unwanted pressure*
- *takeovers (ie of themselves) are more easy*
- *disappearance of mutuality, which could affect image and reputation with customers*
- *a wider range of activities would require higher skills snd could increase personnel and infrastructure costs*
- *risks may be greater*

Unit Three
Financial Markets in the UK

3.1 The role of the Bank of England

As pointed out in the previous Unit, the Bank of England, as the central bank of the UK, is the ultimate supporter of the banking system and ensures that the 'system' always balances. The Bank also uses its intervention in the money markets to influence short-term interest rates. It is necessary to know in some detail how these aims are achieved:

❑ Large transactions between government departments and the private sector result in substantial net flows of money between the Bank of England and the commercial banks, producing temporary surpluses and shortages. Without official intervention these flows of funds through the financial markets would result in volatile interest rates and, on occasions, problems of liquidity for certain institutions.

❑ The Bank of England's operations in the money markets are conducted mainly with the members of the London Discount Market Association (LDMA) who are known collectively as the discount houses. Operations involve the buying and selling of 'eligible' commercial bills of exchange, Treasury bills, local authority bonds, and short-term gilt-edged stock. Eligible bills are those which have been 'accepted' by one of the commercial banks which have been designated as eligible by the Bank of England.

❑ If a shortage emerges during the day, as a result of a net outflow of funds from the banking system, the Bank informs the discount houses that it will buy commercial bills. The houses offer bills to the Bank at prices (and implicitly interest rates) of their own choosing. If the Bank considers these consistent with its current monetary policy aims, (i.e. within the 'undisclosed band' of short-term interest rates it operates) the offers will be accepted and the shortage relieved. Should the rates be too low the Bank will decline to buy bills forcing the LDMA to make further offers at a lower price - implying higher interest rates.

❑ If there is a surplus in the market the bank is able to 'mop-up' the surplus by selling bills and other securities back to the houses, so taking funds out of the system.

❑ In order to influence short-term interest rates selectively, the Bank of England operates in four maturity bands, with dealings normally concentrated in bands 1 and 2:

Band 1	bills with 1-14 days to maturity
Band 2	bills with 15-33 days to maturity
Band 3	bills with 34-63 days to maturity
Band 4	bills with 64-91 days to maturity

These day-to-day activities of the Bank which are meant to influence short-term interest rates and the liquidity of the banking system may be viewed collectively as open-market operations and are an essential part of monetary policy in practice.

The Bank does not deal only with the LDMA. First of all a number of the houses are now owned by banks themselves and there are other institutions such as Gilt Edged Market Makers (GEMMs) and Stock Exchange Money Brokers (SEMBs) who also have direct borrowing facilities from the Bank of England.

Particularly during the corporate tax-gathering season, (i.e. January to April), severe market shortages can occur. At such times the Bank of England will undertake repurchase agreements (REPOS) directly with the commercial banks. The Bank effectively purchases certain securities from the commercial banks (thereby injecting funds into the system) with agreements to sell them back (i.e. for the commercial banks to repurchase them) at a certain date and at an appropriate interest rate.

3.2 The London money markets

The London Discount Market

This market consists of the members of the London Discount Market Association (LDMA) and also includes a few small firms of bill brokers. In 1992 there were nine members. They are in many ways unique institutions and have been regarded as an integral part of the financial mechanism of the City of London. Although their influence (and numbers) has waned , they still have an important role in assisting the Bank of England in its day-to-day objectives in the money markets.

The discount houses deal almost exclusively in short-term funds and instruments. Their business is conducted almost entirely with banks from whom they borrow mainly at call or overnight and thus provide a source of liquidity: placings with members of the LDMA are regarded as high quality liquid assets by the Bank of England.

Dealings are mainly in the following instruments:

- *Treasury bills.* The houses are both primary purchasers of treasury bills as well as providing a secondary market in them.

- *Short-dated government stock, local authority stocks and bonds.*

- *Commercial bills.* The houses are the principal market-makers in bills, discounting and re-discounting eligible, non-eligible bank and trade bills of exchange.

- *Certificates of deposit.* The houses operate a secondary market in CDs, both sterling and currency.

- *Futures, options and swaps.* Greater sophistication of the financial markets has increased the range of short-term instruments for 'hedging' purposes.

The discount houses in the UK act as a 'buffer' between the Bank of England and the banks and help to smooth out temporary shortages and surpluses in the 'system'. The

Bank of England does not normally deal directly with the commercial banks (apart from REPO transactions) but will buy from, and sell to, the discount houses at the various 'band' rates discussed above.

Mainly through the discount houses, then, the Bank of England will attempt to control the supply of credit in the system and the level of short-term interest rates.

The Inter-bank market

This describes an amorphous group of banks and money-brokers who borrow and lend short-term both in sterling and currency. Banks and other financial institutions use the market as a source of funds and also to provide day-to-day liquidity. Transactions are for large amounts and unsecured, with rates based on LIBOR. The market deals almost exclusively in wholesale deposits and loans.

The Certificates of Deposit (CD) market

Sterling CDs are usually issued by banks and building societies for periods of three months to five years. The minimum amount is usually £50,000 and CDs are fully negotiable. Interest rates may be fixed or floating, and CDs may be rediscounted in the secondary market operated by the discount houses. Banks hold other banks' CDs as investments or for liquidity purposes. In many ways, the CD market is merely an extension of the inter-bank market, as banks and building societies use this market as an alternative to the inter-bank market for adjusting their liquidity positions. In London there is also an active market in US dollar CDs.

The local authority market

This is the oldest of the parallel markets, dating back to 1955. Local authorities borrow in the short-term market because interest rates historically are lower than long-term rates. Their reliance on the short-term market largely depends on the cost of alternative finance through Public Works Loan Board. Local authorities also issue loan stock (bonds) and bills which can be bought and sold in the secondary market in which the discount houses are very active.

Local authorities have attempted to increase their sophistication and range of activities in the money markets in recent years. Unfortunately this has not always been successful, and a major legal case involving interest rate swap transactions, which began in mid-1989, has undermined their position in the markets.

The finance house market

Finance houses generally provide funds for instalment credit, i.e. hire purchase finance and leasing. The Finance Houses Association (FHA) was established in 1945 and many of their members now form part of much larger banking groups.

Finance houses raise much of their funds direct from the inter-bank market as well as from commercial companies and the private sector, i.e. retail deposits.

The commercial paper market

First opened in the spring of 1986, the sterling commercial paper market has grown steadily. Commercial paper is short-term debt issued by companies and bought directly by investors. It is negotiable which means it may be traded in the secondary market. There is also a thriving euro-commercial paper market in London.

Commercial paper is the most obvious example of the *securitisation* of bank debt and also *disintermediation*, whereby borrowers and lenders are put into direct contact with each other, with the bank acting as a broker or guarantor for the transaction, i.e. many companies with temporary cash surpluses invest in commercial paper issued by other companies.

The Medium Term Notes (MTNs) market

This market was established in 1990. MTNs represent paper issued for one to five years. Issues can be in a variety of currencies, including the ECU (see Unit 8).

The London International Financial Futures Exchange (LIFFE)

This market opened in September 1982 in the Royal Exchange Building in the City of London. LIFFE provides a medium through which investors and borrowers can hedge against fluctuations in interest rates and exchange rates.

A financial futures contract is defined as a binding agreement between a buyer and a seller to make and take delivery of a fixed quantity and quality of a specified financial instrument or currency upon a fixed or determinable future date.

Terminology of the money markets

The term 'the money markets' traditionally meant just the discount houses. The other markets have often been referred to as the 'parallel' money markets, but even this term appears dated in the 1990s. Markets can describe *participants*, eg the inter-bank markets, or the *products* and *instruments* traded, such as the foreign exchange market, the swaps market, the derivatives market and so on.

The discount market and the 'parallel' sterling markets: some comparisons

- The discount market has a traditional role as the main focus of the Bank of England's daily operations to influence short-term interest rates and to smooth financial flows between government and the banking system.

- Lending in the discount market is mainly on a secured basis, in contrast to the operations of the parallel markets.

- Lender of last resort provision exists only in the discount market and amongst a few market specialists.

- The discount market continues to underwrite the weekly Treasury bill issue .

- The parallel markets (inter-bank and CD) have replaced the discount market as the focus of commercial bank operations to adjust liquidity positions.

3.3 The eurocurrency markets

❑ What is eurocurrency?

❑ Eurocurrencies are bank deposits which are not in the currency of the country in which the bank holding them is located.

❑ Eurodollars are thus defined as dollar deposits with banks outside the US; this would include the overseas offices of American banks.

❑ There are eurocurrencies other than the US dollar, including euro-deutschemarks, euro-French-Francs, euro-Yen and euro-Sterling, but the US dollar still predominates, representing well over half of the total eurocurrency market.

❑ The prefix 'euro' is misleading, since US dollar deposits in Hong Kong and Singapore are also part of the eurocurrency pool: these are often referred to as the Asian dollar market. There are now many financial centres around the world which deal in foreign currency deposits and loans and it is more appropriate to refer to them collectively as the 'off-shore' currency markets, ie as opposed to the 'domestic' currency markets

❑ Sources and uses of eurocurrency funds

❑ Although London is only one of the many eurocurrency markets, it is the largest and is typical. The main *sources of funds* are commercial banks; central banks and international monetary institutions; and overseas residents, individuals as well as corporations. Eurocurrency is raised in the form of straight deposits at LIBID (London Interbank Bid Rate) as well as through the issue of currency certificates of deposit, commercial paper, medium term eurobonds, floating rate notes and other negotiable paper.

❑ The *users of funds* can be governments (often for balance of payments finance); multinational companies (to finance international operations); and commercial banks.

❑ *Maturity transformation* is achieved through the rollover loan whereby a five year commitment may be funded continuously by short-term deposits, usually three or six months; the loan being 'rolled over' and interest adjusted accordingly. Interest rate and currency swaps are also used for this purpose, and for hedging.

❑ Loans are generally priced on the basis of the London Inter-bank offered rate (LIBOR) in the particular currency and term required. Syndicated loans are often rated at 11.00 a.m. London time.

Although LIBOR is the traditional rate quoted, other centres also quote their own rates for eurocurrency loans, e.g. Singapore inter-bank offered rate (SIBOR).

❑ Eurobonds are issued by companies and banks to raise longer-term eurocurrency finance, usually at fixed rates. Floating rate notes involve medium-term financing but based on short-term interest rates. Euro-commercial paper is issued primarily by corporations and is short-term in nature.

The deregulation of the financial markets during the 1980s produced a variety of new financial instruments for both the borrower and the investor in the euromarkets. These included such instruments as revolving underwriting facilities (RUFS), note-issuance facilities (NIFS) and multi-option facilities (MOFS), many of which are already out of fashion. The euromarkets are also the main area of swap activity, both interest rate and currency.

❑ Advantages of using the eurocurrency market

Some of the advantages of using the eurocurrency as opposed to domestic markets have diminished, or disappeared, as the regulatory environment has changed in the past decade or so. Two developments are particularly noteworthy:

❑ *Controls over borrowing in domestic markets* - a prominent feature of monetary control - are now much less in evidence.

❑ *The greater harmonisation of supervisory practices and the extension of reserve and capital adequacy requirements to off-shore deposits* has removed much of the cost advantage previously enjoyed by the eurocurrency markets. The absence of such requirements enabled the euromarkets to operate on finer margins than domestic markets, offering higher rates to depositors and charging less to borrowers.

Nevertheless, the eurocurrency market is large and sophisticated, and still offers advantages to both corporate and financial institutions. It has continued to grow steadily in recent years. The advantages it has over domestic markets are:

- the eurocurrency market provides an opportunity for companies to invest foreign currency surpluses without incurring conversion costs. The funds can subsequently be used for foreign payments;
- the eurocurrency market provides expertise in capital raising and hedging transactions, such as swaps (see Unit 10);
- there are still some tax advantages in dealing off-shore;
- the eurocurrency market provides a large pool of wholesale funds for financial institutions;
- for some banks and securities houses these markets are still the only way in which they can cross institutional boundaries which they are prevented from doing in their own countries - eg by Glass-Steagall in the US and Article 65 in Japan.

3.4 The capital markets

❑ Money markets and capital markets

It could be argued that there is no obvious difference between these two markets. Many large financial institutions have operations and subsidiaries which operate in both. The general distinction is that the capital markets are concerned with longer term or permanent finance, eg bonds and equity, and the money markets concentrate on short-term borrowing and lending.

The last few years also produced a number of new specialist institutions such as Inter-Dealer Brokers, Stock Exchange Money Brokers (SEMBs) and Gilt-Edged Market Makers (GEMMs). GEMMs are important because they also have 'lender of last resort' borrowing facilities from the Bank of England whilst deposits placed with them by banks count as 'primary' liquidity. This is significant if only that it effectively ended the 'unique' position of the discount houses. The role of the GEMMs is important in the Bank of England's funding strategy in the gilt-edged market.

❑ Capital raising

The major 'institution' involved in long term capital raising was traditionally the Stock Exchange itself. However, this no longer exists as a physical presence in one place, and the raising of capital by companies through the issue of ordinary shares (equity) or loan stock now involves a variety of issuing houses, securities trading firms, insurance companies, underwriters, dealers and market makers. Many of these activities are centred in one 'investment bank' which is often owned by a major clearing bank or foreign bank.

Apart from equity, long-term capital is raised in the form of preference shares, debentures and loan stock, i.e. bonds. Since the BIS capital adequacy proposals became generally accepted, commercial banks around the world are now as much interested in capital raising as corporate entities.

The distinction between long and short-term capital (funding) is now less obvious than it used to be. Because of the existence of such products as swaps and options, companies raising long-term funds are able to exchange their fixed interest rate payments for floating rate payments based on short-term interest rates. It is also possible to raise long-term capital in one currency at a fixed rate and convert the interest payments into a floating rate in a completely different currency.

questions and answers

Q 1 Identify the main types of lenders and borrowers in the eurocurrency markets and discuss the characteristics of the markets which have attracted these participants over the past decade.

(Autumn 1985)

Answer

See section 3.3

Q 2 (a) Discuss the role of the parallel sterling money markets in London (15)

(b) Is it still valid to distinguish the parallel markets from the discount market? (10)

(Spring 1988)

Answer

(a) See section 3.2

(b) See section 3.2

Q 3 Discuss the significance of the following in the UK financial system:

(a) the inter-bank market; (9)

(b) commercial (eligible) bank bills; (8)

(c) the Stock Exchange, including reference to changes introduced by 'Big Bang'. (8)

(Spring 1989)

Answer

(a) See section 3.2

(b) See section 3.1

(c) See section 3.4

Q 4 (a) Explain in detail how the Bank of England influences money market rates

(b) To what extent do changes in money market rates lead to changes in

(i) Bank base rates?

(ii) Banks mortgage rates?

(iii) Gilt yields?

(Spring 1992)

Answer

(a) See section 3.1

(b) (i) Interest rates – see Unit 5.2

(iii) Banks mortgage rates are influenced by movements in money market rates, but are not directly linked to base rate and will not rise automatically if money market rates rise. The mortgage market is still dominated by the building societies and, if the banks are to compete, bank mortage rates will reflect societies' rates. Mortgage rates, like base rates, tend to lag changes in money market rates.

(iii) Gilt yields are determined by the supply of and demand for government securities, ie yield varies inversely with price. Changes in wholesale money market rates can influence the gilts market, but there are also other influences such as confidence, changes in expected inflation etc.

Unit Four
The Money Supply

It has already been seen that the supply of money in a modern economy is defined as *currency in circulation* plus *bank deposits*, and in the UK, the *deposits of building societies.*

Notes and coin form a relatively small part of the money supply and the authorities allow changes to reflect the public's requirements. What happens to deposits is therefore the crucial issue in considering the change in the money supply. Three factors are of relevance in determining changes in the level of deposits:

- bank and building society lending to the private sector.
- the public sector borrowing requirement and its financing, or a budget surplus and how this is dealt with
- overseas influences

4.1 Lending to the private sector

This is of great relevance because advances create deposits. When a bank or building society lends money to a customer, the funds ultimately become a deposit of someone else, i.e. the money supply increases. Every loan thus creates a new deposit which in turn can be used as a base for further loans. This process can continue until the total of new deposits created is several times the amount of the original advance. The ability of the banking system to 'create' credit in this way is therefore of great importance in analysing the influence of lending to the private sector on the money supply, and to governments attempting to control the money supply.

❑ The creation of credit

Analysis has traditionally focused on the ability of the banking system to create credit. Since building societies resemble banks in many respects, it is appropriate to include them in the discussion. In considering the power of these financial institutions to create credit, it is essential to bear in mind the environment in which they operate.

There are several practical reasons why their power of credit creation is not unlimited:

1 Banks must maintain non-operational deposits at the central bank equal to a minimum proportion of their deposit liabilities - approximately 0.35% in the UK. Clearing banks must also maintain operational deposits.

2 Banks and building societies must hold a certain proportion of their assets in cash in tills to meet withdrawals.

3 Banks and building societies keep a proportion of their assets in near liquid form - in Treasury bills, certificates of deposit, short-dated gilt-edged stock.

In view of these three factors, for every £100 of new deposits these institutions obtain, assume that they keep some 20% in liquid assets in one form or another. The arithmetic factor by which deposits are increased, the 'credit multiplier', can be calculated by dividing the percentage of the original deposits kept in liquid form into 100. In this case the multiplier will be $100 \div 20 = 5$.

Further limiting factors to the process of credit creation include:

4 There may be insufficient customer demand for loans to carry on the process of credit expansion.

5 The government may impose restrictions on lending.

6 There may be leakages from the system, e.g. overseas or into gilts in which case the funds pass into the government's possession and out of the system.

In order to provide a base for the creation of credit, it is necessary for new money to enter the system. Such funds which constitute the liabilities of the central bank, i.e. notes and banks' operational deposits are sometimes called *high-powered money* since they act as the starting point for the multiple credit creation process to take place. This is in contrast to the money subsequently created *(low-powered money)* which cannot spark off the process. By definition, the only source of high powered money for the banking system as a whole is transactions between the monetary authorities and the commercial banks.

New money may enter the system as a result of any of the following:

- Gilt-edged stock held by the non-bank private sector maturing, involving a transfer of funds to private sector accounts.
- The government may run a budget deficit, e.g. by spending more on building roads or schools without raising taxes or cutting back elsewhere and finance it through the central bank (see section 4.2).

❑ Credit creation: conclusions

- The credit creation process is built on a base of high powered money.
- A certain percentage of assets is held in liquid form.
- The power to create credit is thus not infinite: it is limited to the multiplier which results from the above.
- There are other practical limitations to credit creation such as leakages and demand for loans.

It will be evident from the above that, if the authorities are to regulate the money supply, they will need to control the amount of new money available which might spark off the credit creation process and/or bank lending itself. Methods adopted by the authorities for doing this are discussed in Unit 6.

4.2 The Fiscal Balance

❑ Public Sector Borrowing Requirement

The Public Sector Borrowing Requirement (PSBR) represents the amount to be borrowed each fiscal year by the public sector to make up the shortfall between revenue and expenditure. There are three components:

- Central government budget deficit
- Public corporations' deficit
- Local authorities' deficit

In the UK the size of the PSBR is a major preoccupation of the government. It has attempted to control public spending in order to reduce PSBR. Note that in the UK the sale of public assets (such as British Telecom, British Airways) reduces the size of the PSBR, and this helped the government to achieve its objective in the late 1980s. Note however the massive deterioration in the 1990s as a result of the recession which has depressed tax receipts and increased social security payments.

UK PSBR in relation to GNP

	PSBR (£bn)	% of GNP
1980/81	13.2	5.7
1984/85	10.2	3.1
1986/87	3.3	0.9
1988/89	- 14.4	- 3.0
1990/91	nil	nil
1991/92	13.8	2.3
1992/93 (estimate)	35.0	6.0

Note: a minus PSBR is a PSDR (Public Sector Debt Repayment) - see page 41 for an explanation of this term

❑ Financing the PSBR

This may be done by:

1 Sales of government debt to the *non-bank non-building society private sector.* Government debt consists mainly of gilts, Treasury bills, National Savings, and local authority stocks. The private sector includes persons and companies as well as financial institutions other than banks and building societies.

2 By issuing more cash to the public. (This is a highly inflationary method and is resorted to only by governments who have lost control of their finances).

3 By borrowing from the banking system or the central bank.

4 By borrowing from abroad.

Ignoring no. 2 for the reason stated and no. 4, which is considered later, it can be seen from the following two sections that the impact on deposits (and hence the money supply) of the financing of the PSBR depends on which sector of the economy provides the finance.

❑ Borrowing from the non-bank non-building society private sector

Sales of debt instruments to the non-bank non-building society public will result in a reduction of deposits, since funds will be withdrawn to pay for them. These funds will flow to the government. This initial contraction of funds in the financial system will be offset by the government's increased expenditure elsewhere in the economy, which means that the funds will find their way back into bank and building society accounts. Overall, the impact on the money supply will be negligible.

❑ Borrowing from the banking system or central bank

Any financing of the PSBR by sales of securities (gilts, Treasury bills) to the *banking system* will increase the money supply. Initially the banks' assets will be reshuffled (e.g. certificates of deposit will be sold to pay for gilts). However, when the government spends the money, deposits with banks and building societies will increase.

Sales of stock to the *Bank of England* will also result in an increase in the money supply. As above, when the government spends the money it has received, deposits in the private sector will increase.

4.3 Funding the PSBR

In order to offset the expansionary impact of a PSBR on the money supply, the government (via the Bank of England) will attempt to sell sufficient gilt-edged stock to the non-bank, non-building society private sector to cover the budget shortfall. It is relevant to note that when a budget surplus arises (ie there is a PSDR) because budget receipts exceed expenditure (as happened in the late 1980s) there is a potentially contractionary impact on the money supply. This is offset by purchases of public sector debt (gilts) from the private sector. This action reduces the size of the national debt.

4.4 Overseas influences

So far we have considered only domestic stimuli to monetary expansion. In order to obtain a complete picture, it is necessary to take into account the external flows which might affect the money supply. Because money supply definitions exclude overseas residents' holdings of sterling, it follows that transactions between UK residents and overseas residents will affect the money supply. In total such transactions might result in, for example:

- a current account surplus (increases money supply);
- net bank lending to the overseas sector (increases money supply only if the deposits created end up in UK residents' accounts);
- net government borrowing from overseas (increases money supply only if funds were initially held overseas).

4.5 Money supply changes: summary

We are now in a position to set out the factors which give rise to changes in the money supply in the form of an identity showing the counterparts to change in the M4 definition. The definition M4 is selected since this has been the focus of attention following the reclassification of broad money definitions in 1987.

Counterparts of M4	Effect on M4
(a) Public Sector Borrowing Requirement (PSBR)	+
(b) Sales of public sector debt to the UK non-bank non-building society private sector	-
or	

(a) Public Sector Debt Repayment (PSDR)	–
(b) Purchases of public sector debt from the UK non-bank non-building society private sector	+
and	
(c) increase in sterling lending to the UK private sector	+
(d) change in external and foreign currency counterparts	–
(e) increase in banks' and building societies' net non-deposit liabilities	–

Explanation of changes in M4 counterparts
It is important to explain how each of the changes in M4 counterparts - identified in the table above by the letters (a) to (e) - affects M4:

(a) PSBR - the excess of government spending over revenue - creates new bank deposits and is a net addition to M4.

(b) In order to finance the PSBR/eliminate the PSDR, the government borrows/repays debt. To the extent that its transactions are conducted with the non-bank non-building society private sector, the impact on money supply is neutralised.

(c) A rise in sterling bank lending to the UK private sector increases the money supply since the counterpart to a loan is a deposit.

(d) External and foreign currency counterparts - broadly speaking a balance of payments deficit means that money is flowing out of the country thus reducing the money supply. A balance of payments surplus has the opposite effect.

(e) Non-deposit liabilities such as additional share capital and reserves (retained profits) are not included in the definition of M4, and an increase in these items will reduce financial institutions' deposit liabilities. The net change reflects the increase in non-deposit liabilities less the increase in real assets (such as premises). Overall, the increase in the net non-deposit liabilities of the banks and building societies will reduce the money supply - hence the minus item for this monetary counterpart in the above formula.

4.6 Introduction to techniques for controlling the money supply

Each of the above counterparts to changes in M4 is susceptible to control by the authorities. The following table puts the control of the money supply in perspective, by showing the instruments available alongside the counterpart it can affect. Further discussion of these policy instruments is contained in Unit 6.

Component of change in M4	Instrument
PSBR	Fiscal policy (public sector expenditure and the level of taxation)
Sales of public debt to the non-bank private sector	Debt management Interest rates
Bank and building society lending	Direct controls, ratio controls, interest rates, open market operations
Net external flows	Interest rates

4.7 Changes in the money supply and bank balance sheets

The concept of money supply growth is important to banks because it coincides with growth in deposits, and hence growth in the size of the balance sheet. Of equal significance is the fact that too rapid a rise in money supply can prompt official action - eg credit controls or high interest rates - to slow money supply growth and hence limit banks' balance sheet expansion.

questions and answers

Q1 Outline the main ways in which a government can finance a budget deficit. How might the need to finance a rising deficit affect commercial banks?

(Spring 1986)

Answer

See section 4.2 for the first part. The effect on the banks depends on the method of financing the deficit. e.g. if the government borrows from the banks, bank liquidity is increased and extra lending can take place. Long-term interest rates might rise, affecting banks' lending and profits.

Q2 (a) What is meant by the term 'Public Sector Borrowing Requirement' (PSBR)? (5)

(b) Assuming the PSBR is zero, discuss the factors which could generate an increase in a country's money supply. (11)

(c) Can the credit creation process be carried on indefinitely? (9)

(Spring 1988)

Answer

(a) See section 4.2
(b) See section 4.1, 4.4 and 4.5
(c) See section 4.1

Q3 (a) Define the measure of money supply known in the UK as M4.

(b) Discuss in detail the main factors which cause M4 to grow.

(Spring 1989)

Answer

(a) See section 1.3
Note: questions on changes in the money supply are best approached by reference to the counterparts identity shown in section 4.5
(b) See sections 4.1, 4.2, 4.4, and 4.5

Q 4 In the 1988 UK Budget the Chancellor of the Exchequer indicated that the UK no longer had a Public Sector Borrowing Requirement (PSBR) but a Public Sector Debt Repayment (PSDR).

(a) Explain precisely what the Chancellor meant by this statement (8)

(b) Discuss the impact a PSDR will have on
  (i) interest rates (4)
  (ii) the market for gilt-edged securities (4)
  (iii) the money supply (9)

(Autumn 1989)

Answer

(a) See section 4.2

(b) (i) less pressure for borrowing long-term funds will depress long-term rates

(ii) the gilts market will contract as the government repays debt

(iii) see section 4.2, but apply the arguments in reverse

Q 5 In what ways can the UK government finance its borrowing requirement? (10)

What are the effects on banks' balance sheets of the different methods used? (15)

(Spring 1992)

Answer

See section 4.2

Unit Five
Interest Rates

Interest is essentially the price paid by borrowers to lenders for the use of their money. Borrowing and lending are central to the working of a modern economy and the cost of credit has important effects on the level of consumption and investment as well as a country's exchange rate.

Interest rates play a central part in the day-to-day operation of monetary policy and the Bank of England, through its money market dealings, controls rates at the very short-end of the spectrum. Interest rates are clearly important for the funding of the Public Sector Borrowing Requirement (PSBR) as interest rates may have to rise to make gilt sales and National Savings attractive.

5.1 Real and nominal interest rates

❑ Real rates of interest are the rates actually paid or received (i.e. the nominal rate) adjusted for inflation. If the nominal rate is greater than the rate of inflation then the real interest rate is said to be positive. If inflation is higher than the nominal rate, the real rate is negative.

❑ Real interest rates are calculated most simply by deducting the inflation rate - as measured, say, by the Index of Retail Prices in the UK - from the nominal or 'quoted' rate. For example, if building societies are paying 10% per annum for deposits and inflation is running at 5% per annum, then the depositor is receiving a real return, i.e. above inflation, of some 5%.

This is clearly a very simplistic interpretation, as investors are often more influenced by the expected rate rather than historical rates. The difference between nominal interest rates and the 'expected' rate of inflation may be a more appropriate way of dealing in practice with real rates.

❑ Real interest rates are important, not only as an economic indicator for comparison with other countries, but also because they influence borrower and investor behaviour.

If real rates of interest are positive then companies' costs of borrowing are effectively rising faster than the prices they are able to charge for their own products. Conversely, if real rates are negative, borrowers are encouraged to take on debt whilst investors (i.e. lenders) can see the purchasing power of their savings falling even though the actual amount saved may be greater as a result of the added interest.

❑ During the late 1980s/early 1990s real interest rates were generally high for a number of reasons:

- Governments have operated restrictive monetary policies to combat inflation.
- In Germany, particularly following re-unification, and in some other countries, there have been large budget deficits to finance, intensifying competition for long-term funding. The needs of governments, then, have kept the price of money high.
- Some governments have been reluctant to let the external exchange value of their currencies fall and have defended them by offering high real interest rates. Those countries that are in the Exchange Rate Mechanism (ERM) of the European Monetary System may be forced to raise interest rates to prevent their currencies from falling outside the permitted 'band'.
- Deregulation of interest rates generally around the world and increased competition for savings has arguably resulted in a higher level of rates irrespective of fundamental influences.

5.2 Factors affecting the general level of interest rates

This section is concerned with *why* interest rates move up and down. Whilst there are a number of academic or theoretical explanations associated with such economists as Keynes, the simple approach is that:-

- In the short term interest rates tend to fluctuate in response to *supply and demand influences.*

- *Supply* is determined by day-to-day monetary policy and the credit creation process of the financial system. *Demand* is influenced mainly by borrowers' expectations.

Over the longer term real or 'fundamental' factors are more important, most notably *the rate of inflation:*

- The rate of inflation, in conjunction with the real rate of return investors expect to receive, produces the nominal rate of interest in an economy.

- It is a general (with inevitable exceptions, of course) rule that countries with high inflation tend to have high nominal interest rates, and vice versa.

Interest rates in other countries will, in the absence of exchange control regulations, have an influence on capital flows and hence the supply of funds in the domestic market. Domestic interest rates may need to respond for *exchange rate reasons.*

Short term interest rates are greatly influenced by the authorities through intervention. *Long-term rates*, as stated above, reflect the fundamentals in the economy. However, governments also borrow long-term through the issue of long-dated stock (gilts in the UK) and their needs (or lack of them) can again have an impact on the 'yield curve' which is dealt with on page 51.

❑ Commercial bank base rates

❑ Commercial banks' base rates provide a benchmark for most of their variable rate lending, e.g. 'blue-chip' rate is generally base rate plus 1% or less.

❑ LIBOR lending is usually referred to as wholesale, or 'market related'.

❑ Any bank's lending rates must reflect the cost of raising its funds. If it is to remain in business a bank cannot lend out at a rate below that which it is paying for its deposits.

❑ All interest rates are linked to a greater or lesser degree and the Bank of England's money market dealing rates are central to the whole structure of interest rates. Commercial banks are active in the inter-bank or parallel markets placing funds and, more importantly, borrowing from the markets. Retail deposits have been a declining source of funds (in percentage terms) particularly for the UK clearers, and these deposits have been increasingly supplemented by monies raised directly from the inter-bank market and through the issue of Certificates of Deposit, for example.

❑ The margin between wholesale rates (inter-bank or CDs) and lending rates is of crucial importance. The three month rate is regarded as particularly significant because it is reasonably stable and corresponds to standard money market maturities. Bank base rates have tended to be at, or slightly above, three month inter-bank middle rates.

❑ Consideration is also given to shorter rates (overnight to 7 days) to avoid *arbitrage* against banks. Arbitrage arises when customers are able to borrow on overdraft more *cheaply* than at LIBOR. If this should happen it means that banks are lending at a lower rate than it is costing them to fund the loan. Bank customers might even utilise overdraft facilities to re-lend to banks at money market rates if base rates get too much out of line. This is known as 'round-tripping'.

❑ The pattern of money market interest rates

Why are there so many rates?

It is clear from even a cursory glance at the financial press that there are many rates of interest. Even for similar maturities, say three months, rates can often vary considerably. Why is this so? Apart from the obvious difference between borrowing rates (e.g. LIBOR) and rates for deposits (e.g. LIBID), which is known as the *'spread'*, the main reason is that there are many investors and there are many borrowers. Each has different needs, different credit ratings (risk) and different expectations:

- One would expect a first class bank to pay a lower rate for its funds than an unknown corporate or an individual. Investors are often quite prepared to accept a lower rate of return from one institution because it is seen as a less risky home for his or her savings.

- There are similar considerations with regard to the credit standing of the borrower.
- Expectations are important because both companies and private individuals will have different views of what is going to happen to interest rates in the future.
- Borrowers and investors have different tax positions which invariably change over time. This will influence what a particular investor requires in terms of interest, and also what a borrower is prepared to pay for any maturity.
- Rates will of course vary with the *size* and *time to maturity* of the loan or deposit.
- The currency in which the transaction takes place is an important consideration.

5.3 The yield curve

The yield curve expresses the relationship between interest rates and yields on *similar assets* with different terms to maturity. In 'normal' conditions, short-term interest rates are lower than long-term rates and the yield curve slopes upward and to the right as shown below:

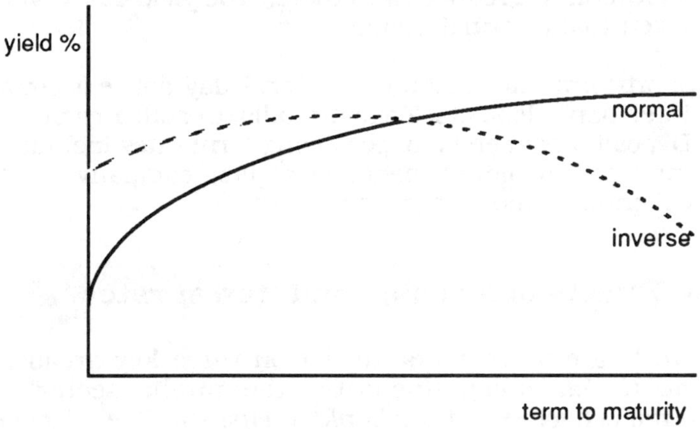

There are essentially two reasons for this. One is that investors of funds require a higher reward for foregoing liquidity and, secondly, risk is generally greater over the longer term. The future is always uncertain and the most important uncertainty is the future level of inflation.

Some investors prefer to hold their money short-term and there are borrowers who also seek short-term funds. Rates up to, say, three months will reflect demand and supply at 'the short end'.

At the other end of the maturity band there will be those investors who wish to lock up funds for a long time at fixed rates, and there will be borrowers who choose longer-term fixed rate finance because of convenience, certainty of cash flow, etc

The day to day relationship between short and long-term rates will depend ultimately on the movement of funds between maturities and this is influenced strongly by expectations:

- Short-term rates may be higher than long-term rates (i.e. an inverse yield curve - see graph on page 51) because borrowers expect rates to fall; conversely, investors will be moving out of the short-term market for the same reason.
- If short-term rates remain high, then funds will eventually flow out of the long-term, raising longer-term rates, whilst the increased supply of funds at the short end will reduce rates there. The yield curve will revert to its 'normal' shape.
- Short-term rates include those on 7 day notice accounts, inter-bank deposits, Treasury bills, Certificates of Deposit, commercial paper. Long-term rates include rates paid on government stock (gilts), company debentures and local authority bonds.

5.4 Effects of a change in interest rates

Interest rate movements impact on three key areas: *the domestic economy* (including the public sector), *the external economy* and *the banking system.* The effects of a *rise* in interest rates are summarised as follows:-

The domestic economy
A rise in interest rates increases the cost of borrowing and makes saving more attractive. This is why interest rates are crucial when governments try to control the level of credit. High interest rates, then, are associated with an increase in personal saving and reduced spending and a reduction in corporate borrowing and investment. A slowdown of economic growth and possibly a recession could result.

The government would normally find it easier to sell gilt-edged securities, not only because of the better interest rate offered, but because purchasers would be tempted by the prospects of a subsequent decline in interest rates and the associated rise in the price of gilts.

The external economy
The effects of a rise in interest rates depends on the relationship to rates in other financial centres. In the short term, money would be attracted by the higher rate which could push up the exchange rate and lead to an increase in foreign exchange reserves. There would be an adverse effect on the invisibles section of the balance of payments since outflows of interest payments would increase.

The banking system
A rise in rates would increase the 'endowment benefit' of low interest demand deposits leading to higher net interest income and profit. This benefit is, however, less significant than it was as retail banks now raise much more of their deposit funds from the wholesale market, as do building societies.

Higher rates may deter borrowing, leading to lower bank advances and smaller bank balance sheets.

The banks' investment portfolios, e.g. gilts and bonds, will fall in value, which could have implications for liquidity as well as profits.

If the rise in rates is part of a general credit squeeze and more company failures then banks would need to increase bad debt provisions.

5.5 Domestic interest rates, eurocurrency rates and exchange rates

❑ There is no essential difference between a dollar held in the US and a dollar held in Europe, i.e. a eurodollar, apart, of course, from its location. The same is true for sterling held in the UK and eurosterling.

❑ The domestic markets and offshore markets are inextricably linked and interest rates in the eurocurrency markets will closely follow rates in the national or domestic markets.

❑ Traditionally rates in the offshore (i.e. eurocurrency) markets have been higher for deposits and lower for loans than in the domestic markets for any particular currency. This has reflected the fact that there have been few reserve or liquidity requirements on offshore business which provides a cost advantage compared with domestic business. This means that banks can afford to pay more for deposits in the euromarkets and charge a lower rate for loans.

❑ The disparity between domestic and offshore interest rates has narrowed considerably in recent years. This reflects first of all the phasing out of exchange control regulations in most developed countries, allowing a free flow of funds between the two markets. Secondly, the imposition of bank capital adequacy requirements, based on total liabilities and assets, in many countries has introduced a degree of regulation where there was none before.

There is clearly a connection between interest rates and spot exchange rates and therefore a very direct relationship between eurocurrency interest rates and spot exchange rates. The connection between interest rates and the forward foreign exchange rate is a little more complicated, as outlined below.

❑ If US dollar interest rates (say for three month deposits) are higher than sterling three month rates, it would be profitable to exchange sterling into dollars and invest it, so long as the exchange rate between sterling and dollars did not move over the period.

❑ Clearly, if the dollar's exchange value against sterling fell between the time the investment was made and its ultimate repayment, the interest advantage over the alternative of remaining and investing in sterling could be completely eroded.

❑ Conversely if the dollar rose in value on the foreign exchanges, the eventual return, after converting back to sterling, would be much greater than the original interest differential expected.

❑ In order to protect against such movements in exchange rates, investors and borrowers take out what is known as forward cover. This means that they sell or buy dollars (or any other major currency) *forward*. By so doing the investor/borrower knows exactly how much sterling is going to be received (or paid away) at maturity.

❑ Forward cover has a cost and, when this cost is added to (or deducted from) the sterling or dollar interest rates, the difference between the two rates is then very small, or in fact nothing. Those investors/borrowers who do not cover their deals forward in this way are taking a gamble on what is going to happen to spot exchange rates in the future: they are speculating.

Currency	*Eurocurrency rates (3 months)*	*Cost of forward cover against US dollar (3 months)*
Sterling	9.875	5.78
US dollar	4.0	–
Swiss franc	9.25	5.3
French franc	10.00	6.06
Japanese yen	4.75	0.56

Rates (expressed as % p.a.) as at June 1992

In the example above, a holder of US dollars could earn more interest by exchanging his dollars and investing in sterling, Swiss Francs, French Francs, or even Yen.

❑ However, on the foreign exchanges, forward Swiss and French Francs, Yen and sterling are all at a discount against the US dollar and when the cost of covering forward is deducted, e.g. 10.00 – 6.06 for French Francs, the holder of US dollars would be no better off.

The example above seems to imply that there is no advantage in switching between currencies on a fully covered basis. However, the markets are fluctuating continuously; some are open when others are not and there is always news being released which may be good for some currencies but not for others. Finally, whenever a group of investors has a view of interest rates or exchange rates, there will always be another group which takes an opposite view.

questions and answers

Q1 Evaluate the effect of an increase in a country's interest rates on:
(a) its commercial banks;
(b) its balance of payments.

(Autumn 1985)

Answer
See section 5.4.

Q2 (a) What is meant by 'real' rates of interest, and how are they calculated?
(b) Why have real rates remained high in most major economies?

(adapted from Spring 1986)

Answer
(a) See section 5.1.
(b) Government policies to curb inflation; the need to finance large budget deficits; to defend exchange rates.

Q3 (a) Why are there so many rates of interest in a developed economy? (15)
(b) Describe how these different rates of interest are illustrated by the operations of a commercial bank. (10)

(Spring 1987)

Answer

(a) See section 5.2.

(b) A commercial bank's business contains the whole range of factors. On the deposit side, interest paid on accounts ranges from current balances with only notional interest to fixed term wholesale deposits. On the asset side the operations range from wholesale short-term low risk lending to loans for smaller amounts, for longer periods, and carrying greater risk.

Q 4 (a) For what reasons might a government seek to raise the level of interest rates in the economy? (11)

(b) Examine in detail how the authorities in the UK influence the level of interest rates. (14)

(Autumn 1989)

Answer

(a) See section 5.4

(b) See section 3.1 (Note: the authorities seek mainly to influence short-term rates, leaving long-term rates to market forces).

Q 5 (a) What is a yield curve?

(b) Why is upward sloping yield curve considered normal?

(c) To what extent does the shape of the yield curve depend on expectations about the future?

(Spring 1992)

Answer

(a) See section 5.3

(b) See section 5.3

(c) See section 5.3

Unit Six
Economic Policy

6.1 Aims and objectives of economic policy

Economic policy refers to the techniques or measures used by governments in seeking to attain their overall economic objectives - ie to achieve a satisfactory performance in the following areas:

Inflation
All governments have been concerned to maintain the internal purchasing power of the currency, albeit with varying degrees of success. Rising prices harm those living on fixed incomes, can cause labour unrest and harm the balance of payments by making the country's exports less competitive abroad and imports more attractive to domestic customers.

Employment
A high and stable level of employment is an accepted objective of all governments and political parties.

Balance of payments
A prolonged period of current account deficits increases a country's reliance on foreign borrowing and pushes down the exchange rate. Conversely, surpluses impact on the domestic money supply and can be inflationary. The underlying aim is for equilibrium over the longer term rather than a balance on current account every year.

Economic growth
If an economy is growing, i.e. Gross National Product (GNP) is increasing, then there is a bigger 'cake' to share amongst the population. The standard of living improves.

Not everyone, however, shares the cake equally, and one of the problems of economic policy is to achieve the necessary rate of growth whilst also achieving an equitable distribution of wealth.

❑ Conflicts in achieving these objectives

Economic policy often fails to achieve its objectives because these are rarely attainable simultaneously. Policies can often achieve some aims only to the detriment of others. For example:-

- Economic growth is often stimulated by a policy of credit expansion and greater consumer spending. Too great an expansion, however, can cause inflation.

- Increased demand by the personal or corporate sector, whilst stimulating economic growth, may encourage imports and reduce the number of goods available for export, producing a balance of trade deficit.

- Rising prices and a deficit on the current account of the balance of payments may be controlled by measures such as a credit squeeze and curbs on government expenditure. These, however, reduce demand, purchasing power and ultimately production. Lower production implies lower economic growth and possibly unemployment.

- It is clear that governments have to compromise between the various objectives of economic policy and establish priorities which may ultimately be politically determined.

6.2 Monetary policy

❑ Targets of monetary policy

One of the major elements of economic policy is monetary policy. Such policy involves the government in attempting to achieve certain *targets* (sometimes called the *intermediate targets* of monetary policy).

❑ The main intermediate target of monetary policy is the *money supply* and its rate of growth. We should remember from Unit 1 that there are several definitions and only one or two of them may be targeted specifically.

❑ Other targets could include the *exchange rate.* The authorities might attempt to hold the exchange rate within a predetermined relationship with other currencies, e.g. full membership of the Exchange Rate Mechanism (ERM) of the European Monetary System.

❑ Controlling the growth in *credit.* Monetary control in the UK has often been concerned with limiting the demand for, and availability of, credit. The major source of credit, both personal and corporate, has traditionally been provided through the banking system. Finance houses, and, more recently, building societies, also provide finance directly to the general public.

Credit 'squeezes' followed by periods of relative laxity have been used to curb or encourage the level of demand in the economy.

❑ *Interest rates* are also another obvious and important target of monetary policy. The key role of interest rates is considered below.

❑ The cost of credit (interest rates)

❑ The cost of credit has played a major role in controlling the level of demand. In theory, *higher interest rates* should encourage personal saving and reduce spending, leading to a lower level of demand. At the same time companies will be deterred from borrowing and will cut back on investment, so production will fall.

❑ Lowering *interest rates* has the opposite effect, leading to an expansion of demand (lower savings), increased corporate borrowing and ultimately a higher level of production and economic activity.

❑ Interest rates may also be used to influence the *exchange rate* and to push it in a particular direction, notably in the pound's case in recent years to keep the currency in its permitted bands within the ERM.

❑ In reality the relationship between interest rates and credit or the level of economic activity is difficult to quantify and is far from certain:

- People may borrow even if interest rates rise, particularly if the money is to be used to purchase goods which are rapidly rising in price.

- Companies may continue to borrow at higher rates if they fear that credit will not be available at all in the near future, or for 'distress' borrowing if profits are eroded as a result of the credit squeeze.

- Low rates of interest may not act as a stimulant to the economy; consumers and producers alike may be pessimistic about the future, e.g. loss of job or continued recession in the home country and abroad.

❑ Techniques of monetary policy

The following are the methods by which governments, through their central banks, influence the monetary policy targets indicated above:

Central bank dealing rates
All central banks act as lenders of last resort to their own domestic commercial banks and in many countries the *discount rate* is the typical rate at which they are prepared to lend to banks in their role as ultimate providers of liquidity to the banking system.

❑ Most central banks, such as the US Federal Reserve and the Bank of Japan, lend directly to the commercial banks which may involve the discounting of bills of exchange.

❑ In the UK, the Bank of England provides assistance to the money markets and the banking system mainly via the discount houses. The price of such assistance has been determined since the early 1980s by intervention rates.

❑ The central bank discount rate (or the rate at which the central bank 'intervenes' in the market) is usually regarded as the fulcrum of the whole interest rate structure in the short-term markets and, by varying the terms or the rate at which it is prepared to provide support, the central bank can move the whole spectrum of interest rates up or down.

❑ Central bank discount intervention rates also have

psychological and political importance in that movements can often indicate a change of government policy and are particularly significant because of their impact on foreign exchange rates.

❑ In the UK, an increase in the Bank of England's intervention rates will lead to a rise in inter-bank rates which could well push up clearing bank base rates and the mortgage rate. Creating a surplus in the money markets, accompanied by lower intervention rates, will lead to a fall in interest rates generally.

Open-market operations

Open-market operations involve the buying and selling of government securities and commercial bills of exchange by the central bank with the object of influencing interest rates, the availability of credit in the system and ultimately the money supply.

Such securities include Treasury bills as well as the more common longer term gilt-edged government stock. The Bank of England (and the US Federal Reserve) also undertake repurchase transactions (REPOS) with the money market, involving the sale and repurchase of securities at pre-determined rates of interest.

❑ Open-market operations (including REPOS) have two main effects:

- *On interest rates.* If the central bank sells securities on the 'open market' this will depress their price and yields automatically rise. Purchases of gilts on the other hand may raise their price and lead to lower yields. Short-term interest rates can be influenced (as explained in Section 3.1)

- *On bank credit.* If government securities are sold to the public (i.e. the non-bank private sector) money passes from the banking system to the central bank. Commercial banks' short-term, ie 'liquid' assets are *reduced* and they may have to reduce their lending which will eventually work through to bank deposits (i.e. via credit creation) and the money supply.

If securities are bought *from* the public by the central bank, cash is injected into the banking system and commercial banks are then able to lend more.

Ratios and reserve requirements
Many central banks impose some sort of reserve requirements on their commercial banks; these requirements involve the maintenance by the banks of specific assets in relation to deposit liabilities:

- Some countries use minimum cash ratios supplemented by minimum holdings of designated *liquid* assets, usually including Treasury bills or other government securities and eligible paper such as commercial bills. Such assets (apart from cash, of course) may or may not be interest-bearing.

- By influencing the supply or cost of holding such *reserve assets* (using open-market operations, for example) the central bank can influence the commercial banks' ability to lend and ultimately the money supply.

- Reserve requirements and the ratios themselves can periodically be changed by the central bank.

Special deposits
The Bank of England has used special deposits at various times to reduce excess liquidity in the banking system and thus restrain lending. Under this system commercial banks are forced to deposit money with the central bank to be held in a special fund which cannot be included as part of their liquid funds for monetary control purposes.

Direct controls
Direct controls usually fall into areas which directly affect a financial institution's ability to make loans or to attract deposits:-

- *Quantitative controls* on lending, i.e. the setting of a *ceiling* level for the overall growth in a bank's advances.

- *Qualitative controls* on lending, i.e. imposing limits on certain areas to which institutions can lend whilst actively encouraging lending to other areas of the economy such as small businesses, agriculture, strategic industries.

- *Controls on deposits*, i.e. limiting the total amount of deposit liabilities which can be raised from a particular sector. Building societies, for example, are constrained by the amount they can raise in *wholesale* funds.

❑ Monetary policy and the banking system

Monetary policy has a direct impact on the banking system:

❑ The imposition of higher interest rates, reserve requirements, or direct controls will restrict growth in the balance sheet.

❑ Changes in interest rates can affect bank profitability (see section 5.4).

❑ The level of interest rates can be affected by
 (i) the size of the PSBR (a large PSBR tends to raise long-term rates to make gilt sales attractive);
 (ii) direct central bank intervention.

6.3 Fiscal policy

The other major element of economic poicy is fiscal policy, which refers to how the economy is controlled through budgetary means. Aggregate - or total - demand and supply in the economy is managed by fiscal policy through varying the levels of government overall revenues and expenditure, and specifically through taxation policies.

Fiscal policy determines how much (if anything) the government will have to borrow to balance expenditure with receipts. The borrowing requirement (PSBR) provides the essential link between monetary policy and fiscal policy, since the method of financing the PSBR has a key role in the growth of the money supply. Government borrowing is a function of its expenditure plans less revenue from taxes and other sources. It is not always a negative figure, and from the late 1980s the UK government's receipts often exceeded its expenditure (partly helped by the privatisation strategy and the sales of public sector assets) resulting in Public Sector Debt Repayment (PSDR) and the repurchase of some government debt (gilt-edged stock) from the public.

Fiscal policy can be aimed at the 'macro' level of the economy in order to influence the level of total production and employment, i.e. the Keynesian approach to demand management. However, the very size of government expenditure and the way it is financed (taxation, customs and excise, borrowing) also has important indirect effects on the level of demand in the economy. Here we refer to such items of expenditure as state pensions, unemployment benefits and subsidies which are all effectively transfer payments.

Taxation also impacts in an indirect way, reflecting the difference between direct taxes (taxes on income) and indirect taxes (taxes on consumption/spending). VAT and duties on, say, alcohol and tobacco products, form part of government revenue, but can also be used to influence consumer spending patterns.

6.4 Prices and incomes policy

Use of this policy relates to government attempts to limit rises in retail prices and wages either by directive or through voluntary restraint. Such policies have been tried many times and in many countries, from the Third World to the developed economies of Western Europe. They are rarely successful in the medium or long term.

6.5 Exchange rate policy

During the late 1980s a number of governments around the world became increasingly interested in collaborating to influence exchange rates. The Group of Seven (G7) countries, in particular, saw a need to reduce wide fluctuations in exchange rates in the interests of world trade harmonisation, and also because increasing deregulation of financial markets worldwide had liberated capital flows. The virtual abandonment of exchange control regulations in most developed countries has meant that capital has become truly international and can flow freely to wherever it can earn the highest reward commensurate with risk.

In principle, the desired level of a country's exchange rate represents a balance between ensuring that export potential is maximised (i.e. a low exchange rate) against the dangers of importing inflation from abroad. (A low exchange rate makes imports more expensive and can easily impact on prices in the home market, particularly if imports are mainly raw materials and semi-manufactured goods).

Exchange rate policy for ERM members (all members of the EC except Greece) is geared to ensuring that their currencies remain within their agreed bands in the system (see section 8.6).

6.6 The effectiveness of economic policy

The limitations of economic policy were outlined at the beginning of this Section mainly in terms of its objectives, which are rarely achieved in unison in any country.

The *targets* of both monetary and fiscal policy (as well as other forms of government intervention) also limit their effectiveness, as do the various *techniques* employed, e.g.

❑ Money supply is not easy to define and thus even more difficult to measure or control.

❑ Interest rates have proved to be a blunt weapon and do not always produce the expected response, particularly in the short term.

❑ Exchange rates are volatile, and setting the target rate itself - i.e. to protect the balance of trade whilst avoiding inflation - is somewhat subjective. One of the biggest debates before the UK joined the Exchange Rate Mechanism of the EMS in October 1990 was the 'correct' level for sterling.

❑ Managing total demand in the economy through budgetary means is difficult if only because the government is involved in spending a great deal of money in actually running the country. This money has to be raised in taxes, and limits the degree of flexibility in 'fine-tuning' the economy.

❑ The relationship between the central bank and the commercial banks is very important and the regulatory authorities must be able to rely on a positive response from the banking system as a whole to any directive. It usually follows that the central bank will have a monopoly of the note-issue and act as banker to the commercial banks and as lender of last resort.

One of the issues facing the European Community as it moves towards Economic and Monetary Union is the organisation and function of a European Central Bank: where it should be located ; what powers it should have; and its relationship with national central banks.

Economic policy : conclusion

The effectiveness of economic policy, however it is implemented, will in the end depend upon how realistic any government's aims are and an acceptance that not all objectives can be achieved at once.

questions and answers

Q 1 In seeking to achieve the ultimate objectives of monetary policy, the authorities can set *intermediate* targets.

(a) Discuss the *intermediate* targets that might be selected (17)

(b) List the techniques that could be used to achieve these targets (8)

(Spring 1989)

Answer

(a) See section 6.2

(b) See section 6.2

Q 2 (a) State the main objectives of economic policy. (4)

(b) Why in practice is it difficult to achieve these objectives simultaneously? (9)

(c) To what extent have each of the main economic objectives been achieved in the UK in the past decade? (12)

(Autumn 1989)

Answer (updated to 1992)

(a) See section 6.1

(b) See section 6.1

(c) Economic growth: satisfactory preformance in mid/late 1980's with growth averaging around 3% p.a. in line with European average. Inferior performance in period 1990-92.

Inflation: performance quite good in mid 1980s (4%-5%) deteriorating towards the end of the decade (8%) - well above the EC average, before moving down to the EC average in 1990.

Unemployment: rose to almost 3 million in 1992.

Balance of payments: current account moved fom a small surplus in the early 1980s to a massive deficit (£20 billion) in 1989. Some improvement during recession of 1990s to a deficit of £10 billion.

Q3 In recent years the UK Government has relied very heavily on high interest rates to achieve its economic objectives.

(a) Identify the particular economic objectives at which this policy was aimed. (4)

(b) To what extent has the policy succeeded in effecting an improvement in the objectives you have identified in (a)? (6)

(c) Discuss the policy alternatives that could have been adopted to help achieve the Government's economic objectives. (15)

(Spring 1991)

Answer

(a) Inflation (10% in 1989); current account (–£20bn in 1989)

(b) Inflation down sharply in 1992 (4%); current account deficit halved, but still large given the recessionary background.

(c) See sections 6.3, 6.4, and 6.5.

Q4 (a) Why and how do governments seek to control the level of demand? (16)

(b Which methods of control has the UK Government relied on since October 1990? (9)

(Spring 1992)

Answer

(a) Why - see section 6.1; how - see sections 6.2 to 6.5

(b) High interest rates and exchange rate policy through ERM membership have been the methods used.

Unit Seven
The Balance of Payments

7.1 Structure of balance of payments

The balance of payments is a record of a country's external financial transactions in a given period, usually a calendar year. The accounts consist of:

- Transactions in visible goods
- Transactions in services
- Capital transactions
- Balancing item, i.e. unidentified flows
- The change in reserves

The table on the following page shows the UK's position in recent years. It is important to know the individual items comprising the accounts, and the broad trends in trade and the current account, but the *detailed figures are included for illustrative purposes only.*

Notes to the balance of payments table

❑ The balancing item at the bottom of the table (marked with an asterisk*) represents errors and omissions in recording entries. It is a balancing item only in the sense that it registers the difference between the total value of recorded transactions and the actual flow of money identified by the authorities. This has been one the largest items on the UK's balance of payments in recent years. The category is not introduced to 'make the balance of payments balance'.

❑ Nevertheless, the balance of payments always does balance, because total currency flows considered above, i.e. the sum of items A to D equals the change in reserves.

❑ The official UK balance of payments presentation shows

item E (changes in reserves) as part of "net transactions in assets/liabilities." It is shown separately here in order to emphasise its role in financing a current account deficit when all other capital flows have been taken into consideration (see section 7.4), or as in the UK's case in 1987, for example, showing the effect of capital inflows in excess of those required to offset the current account shortfall.

UK Balance of Payments

	1985 £bn	1987 £bn	1989 £bn	1991 £bn
Visible trade				
Exports	78.0	79.4	92.5	103.7
Imports	81.1	90.3	116.7	113.8
Visible balance (A)	- 3.1	- 10.9	- 24.2	- 10.1
Invisibles (net)				
Government services	- 1.3	- 1.6	- 2.3	- 2.4
Transport and travel	+ 0.4	- 2.2	- 2.8	- 3.1
Services (insurance, banking etc.)	+ 7.6	+ 9.5	+ 9.8	+11. 0
Interest, profits and dividends	+ 2.8	+ 5.0	+ 4.0	+ 1.6
Transfers (mainly to EC budget)	- 3.0	- 3.4	- 4.6	- 1.4
Invisible balance (B)	+ 6.3	+ 7.3	+ 4.1	+ 5.7
Current account balance	+ 3.2	- 3.6	- 20.1	- 4.4
Capital flows (net)				
Investment (direct and portfolio)	- 17.3	+ 2.7	- 22.4	- 7.3
Transactions of banks	+ 7.6	+ 2.5	+ 16.9	+ 9.0
Other identified flows	+ 2.0	- 0.9	+ 12.7	+ 4.4
Total capital flows (C)	- 7.7	+ 4.3	+ 7.2	+ 6.1
*Balancing item * (D)*	+ 6.3	+ 11.3	+ 7.5	- 4.4
*Total **A** to **D** = **E** (change in reserves)*	+ 1.8	+ 12.0	+ 5.4	- 2.7

**See note on previous page relating to item (D)*

7.2 The current account

The balance of trade

This represents the difference between a country's earnings from merchandise exports and the payments it makes for imports.

The UK has traditionally experienced a deficit on visible trade, but the early 1980s saw a surplus when North Sea oil revenues peaked. Since then the account has returned to deficit.

Terms of trade

The terms of trade of a country express the relationship between two sets of prices

- prices which are paid for imports, and
- prices received for exports

A rise in the price of exports relative to imports indicates an improvement in the terms of trade. For example, if over a period a country's terms of trade are seen to have improved by 10%, this means that export prices have risen by 10% more than import prices, in other words, 10% *less exports in volume* would have been needed to purchase the *same amount of imports*. The calculation is made according to the following formula:

$$\frac{\text{export price index (weighted for different products)}}{\text{import price index (weighted for different products)}} \times 100$$

An improvement in the terms of trade need not necessarily lead to a corresponding improvement in a country's balance of trade. The effect will depend on the respective elasticities of demand for the goods exported and imported. If, for example, higher export prices lead to a more than proportionate reduction in the amount of goods exported, because demand is elastic, the effect on the balance of trade of an improvement in the terms of trade would be unfavourable. Only if the quantities of goods traded remained largely unchanged (because demand was inelastic) would there be a corresponding improvement in the trade balance after a rise in the terms of trade.

Another example of the effect of a movement in the terms of trade on the trade balance can be seen from a devaluation or downward float which moves the terms of trade downward. In the short term this makes imports dearer and exports cheaper, thus producing a deterioration in the trading position; but in the longer term, if the price elasticities are positive, imports will be reduced and exports stimulated and the balance of payments will improve - the so-called *J-curve* effect.

Invisible trade

Invisible trade is mainly concerned with the import and export of services. These include:

- Banking and financial services.
- Transport services - civil aviation, shipping costs.
- Government services, including payment for troops stationed abroad, consular services.
- Interest, profits and dividends: all investment income received or paid in respect of profits, dividends and interest.
- Travel: all spending by residents abroad and by visitors.
- Transfers, remittances, including official transfers to the EC budget.

Importance of the current account position

The sum of visible trade and invisible trade produces the current account balance. The concept is important because, being a record of all current transactions, it shows the extent to which the country is paying its way or living beyond its means as the case might be.

7.3 The capital account

This section of the accounts consists of the following:

Investments and other capital flows

These include:

- Official long-term capital - essentially inter-government loans plus subscriptions to certain international organisations.

- Overseas *portfolio investment* in government stocks, local authority bonds, issues by public corporations and company shares, plus *direct investment* by foreign companies setting up subsidiaries or acquiring production facilities

- private investment overseas - direct investment plus investment in shares of foreign-based companies or overseas government bonds (portfolio investment).

- Net overseas currency borrowing or lending by banks.

- Import credit and export credit.

7.4 Financing and rectifying current account deficits

❑ Financing the deficit

It can be seen from the table in section 7.1 that a current account deficit can be *financed* by net capital inflows. These inflows may be:

- Short-term capital flows attracted by high real interest rates. A current account shortfall can effectively be covered in this way, but such inflows - 'hot money' - can easily be reversed, leaving the balance of payments in a vulnerable position.

- Portfolio investment (see section 7.3).

- Direct investment (see section 7.3)

- Borrowing from abroad by the private sector.

- Borrowing from abroad by the government (to cover any shortfall arising from the fact that the current account deficit is larger than the inflow from other capital sources and from drawing down reserves (see below).

In addition to, or as an alternative to capital inflows, the government can draw on its holding of *international reserves* to finance a current account deficit. A country's reserves consist of:

- gold
- convertible currencies
- facilities with the International Monetary Fund (IMF)

In practice, it is holdings of currencies that constitute the *pool of liquidity on which countries draw in order to finance a balance of payments deficit, or to intervene on the foreign exchanges to support currencies (see Unit 8).* The most important currency is still the US dollar, but a long-term trend has seen the deutschmark and the yen assume a more prominent role.

Official holdings of foreign exchange

	1981 %	1988 %	1990 %
US Dollars	71.5	64.7	56.4
Pounds Sterling	2.1	2.8	3.2
Deutschmarks	12.8	15.7	19.7
Japanese Yen	4.0	7.7	9.1
Other	9.6	9.1	11.6

Gold continues to account for a large proportion of total international reserves, but countries' gold holdings tend to remain fairly stable.

Facilities with the IMF consist of:

- Special Drawing Rights (SDRs) - an international reserve asset created in the late 1960s when there were fears of a shortage of international liquidity. SDRs account for only 2% of total reserves.

- Reserve position in the IMF, representing an automatic drawing right on the IMF.

International Liquid Assets (as at the end of April 1992)

	$bn	%
Gold (valued at $336 per oz)	316	25
Currencies	887	70
SDRs	27	2
Reserve position at IMF	36	3
Total International Reserves	1266	100

❑ Rectifying the deficit

A prolonged deficit on current account or a continued outflow of capital cannot be financed indefinitely. There is a limit to what one country can borrow, and the reserves obviously will eventually run out.

The time will come when action has to be taken to *rectify* the current account deficit.

Monetary and fiscal policy
If the adverse balance is caused by inflation making exports less competitive abroad, while at the same time excessive demand is causing imports to flow in rapidly, then measures to reduce inflationary tendencies and demand are needed - a credit squeeze or deflation. Measures which may be taken are:

- Raising interest rates to encourage saving and discourage borrowing which may be used to pay for imports.
- Open-market operations.
- Directives to the banks on lending.
- Hire purchase restrictions.
- Budgetary (fiscal) measures to reduce demand by higher taxation or reduced government spending using particular taxes or subsidies to stimulate exports.
- Prices and incomes policy.

Exchange rate adjustment

With a system of floating rates of exchange the government can encourage a fall in the rate; this is known as *depreciation of the currency*, whereas under fixed exchange rates (such as the ERM) it involves a formal *devaluation*.

Depreciation/devaluation involves a reduction in the exchange value of a country's currency in relation to other currencies. The effect is to make the exports of the depreciating country cheaper to foreign buyers while imports become more expensive in terms of the depreciated currency.

Depreciation of the currency in the short-term has an adverse effect on the balance of trade, but in the long run the balance of trade should improve (the J-curve effect). There are, of course, difficulties:

- Imports of food and raw materials are essential and will now cost more.
- Devaluation or depreciation is automatically inflationary and this could result in higher wage demands and even more inflation.
- Domestically produced goods will be diverted to the export market and this together with the fall in imports will leave less goods for the home market. Unless excessive demand is held down or production increased, then again inflation may result.
- Elasticities of demand for imports or for exports may not be high enough to produce the desired improvements in the trade balance.

See above for the J-curve effect of the impact of devaluation of the currency on the trade account and the effect of elasticity of demand for imports and exports.

Direct controls over imports

This means improving the visible trade balance by raising import duties or imposing restrictions such as import deposits. Disadvantages are:

- Other countries may retaliate.

- Restricting other people's exports (our imports) makes them less able to pay for our exports (their imports).

- It is difficult to limit the import of food, oil or raw materials, particularly if the latter are needed for increased production of exports.

- The UK is a member of the General Agreement on Tariffs and Trade (GATT) which aims to reduce tariff barriers generally in the interests of world trade.

questions and answers

Q1 (a) Explain the significance to a country of the performance of its balance of payments on the current account. (9)
(b) Is an adjustment of the exchange rate sufficient to rectify a sizeable deficit on a country's current account? What other measures could be introduced? (16)

(Spring 1986)

Answer

(a) See section 7.2.
(b) If exports and imports are highly price elastic, an exchange rate adjustment would be effective on its own. Otherwise a deflation package would be necessary to reinforce the devaluation. See section 7.4.

Q2 If the balance of payments always balances, how can a balance of payments deficit arise?

(Autumn 1986)

Answer

This question refers to the structure of the balance of payments and the fact that it consists of several parts, any of which (the trade account, the current account) can be in deficit. The overall balance of payments (A to D in the table in section 7.1) is matched by equal and opposite flows from changes in the reserves.

Q 3 (a) Distinguish between a country's 'balance of trade' and its 'terms of trade'.

(b) To what extent can a government influence its balance of trade and its terms of trade?

(Autumn 1987)

Answer

(a) See sections 7.1 and 7.2.

(b) The balance of trade can be influenced by policy measures - for example to effect an improvement, devaluation, deflation, and import controls. Terms of trade are largely determined by price developments in world markets, but devaluation or revaluation can have an impact.

Q 4 (a) Explain briefly how a current account deficit can be
(i) financed (4)
(ii) reduced (9)

(b) What effects does the UK's membership of the Exchange Rate Mechanism (ERM) have on the Government's ability to
(i) finance a current account deficit? (4)
(ii) reduce a current account deficit? (8)

(Spring 1992)

Answer

(a) See section 7.4

(b) (i) Ability to finance a deficit is increased through official access to short and medium term facilities to support currency

(ii) ERM membership removes devaluation option as a means of reducing a current account deficit. Deflation of the economy by tightening monetary policy may be precluded if this is likely to result in upward pressure on the exchange rate, taking currency above its upper limit in its ERM band.

Unit Eight
Exchange Rates

8.1 Operation of the market

Although foreign exchange activity takes place in almost every country at some level, the major foreign exchange markets are located in the world's financial centres including London, Frankfurt, New York, Tokyo, Hong Kong and Singapore. Brokers are important in bringing the various 'players' together, i.e. matching buyers and sellers. The main participants in the markets are:

Commercial banks
Banks act on behalf of their clients and customers at all levels, from the tourist who wishes to purchase currency to the corporation involved in international trade transactions or investments in another country. Banks also operate on their own account and some make sizeable profits from their foreign exchange activities.

Corporations
International trade usually involves payments or receipts of currency other than the one used in the company's own country. Corporate treasurers are concerned to obtain or sell foreign currency at the best price without creating an exchange 'exposure'. Foreign investment such as the purchase of an overseas subsidiary or associate involves foreign exchange, both at the time of purchase and when profits are eventually repatriated to the parent company.

The central banks
Most central banks are responsible for holding their country's gold and currency reserves for balance of payments financing and intervening in the foreign exchange markets. From the end of the Second World War until the early 1970s currencies moved within strict limits set by the IMF. 1973 saw a general trend towards freely floating exchange rates, but from the end of the 1970's the

European Monetary System (EMS) re-imposed a degree of discipline over currency fluctuations, involving those countries who participate in the Exchange Rate Mechanism (ERM), including the UK from October 1990. Central banks, in or outside of the ERM. generally try to prevent large movements, either up or down, in the external value of their country's currency, partly to maintain an orderly market, but also as part of overall economic policy. Central bank members of the ERM, of course, are duty bound to intervene in the currency markets.

8.2 Factors affecting exchange rates

❑ Medium and long-term movements

There are three economic factors which cause exchange rates to move over the long term. These *economic fundamentals* are:

Relative rates of inflation
If one country experiences faster inflation than another, then the exchange rate of the country with higher inflation will in the long run fall relative to the currency of the second country. The *theory of purchasing power parity* explains why this is true. A higher rate of inflation will have to be countered over a period by a roughly proportionate fall in the exchange rate, to restore equilibrium in real purchasing power.

Balance of payments performance
A persistent deficit on current account (i.e. payments for imports of goods and services exceed receipts for exports) implies a higher demand for other countries' currencies on the exchanges than for the domestic currency. The exchange rate should fall (again over the long term) provided the current account shortfall is not continually offset by equal capital inflows. Even then, a persistent current account deficit would probably generate a lack of confidence, causing the exchange rate to fall.

Relative interest rates
Changes in interest rate differentials between countries result in different patterns of international capital flows. Funds will tend to move (other things such as inflation

being equal) to currencies offering higher interest rates. This will increase demand for the currencies concerned, raising or supporting the exchange rate

❑ Short term movements

Changes in indicators relating to the economic fundamentals can exert a significant short-term impact on exchange rates. For example, announcement of a better than expected month's trade surplus, or a lower than expected monthly inflation rate can cause the exchange rate to appreciate. Exchange rates also react in the short-term to:

- *Direct intervention by the authorities,* such as a central bank purchasing its own currency on the foreign exchanges.
- *Changes in economic policies,* e.g. an announcement that monetary policy is to be tightened might lead to a strengthening of the exchange rate.
- *Political developments,* such as the announcement of a general election, industrial unrest, outbreak of war.
- *Expectations.* Expectations of a fall in a currency's value will lead to selling by holders, actually producing a depreciation.

8.3 Exchange rate systems

Over the past twenty years the international monetary system has moved from a period of fixed exchange rates (1945-1973) through a period of generalised floating and then in certain areas a return to a more managed approach, most obviously represented by the Exchange Rate Mechanism of the European Monetary System.

❑ Fixed exchange rates

Until 1971, members of the International Monetary fund (IMF) had agreed to peg their exchange rates to the US dollar. Currencies were allowed to fluctuate within a rigorous band of only 1% either side of the agreed par against the dollar. The dollar itself was convertible into gold at US$35 per fine ounce. Governments were bound to take steps to maintain the parity of their own currencies by all the means at their disposal. Direct intervention involved buying or selling their own currency using gold or foreign currency reserves. Indirect methods involved monetary and fiscal policies. If these measures failed, a formal agreement with the IMF to adjust the exchange rate was necessary as a last resort.

The system broke down in the early 1970s largely because the US dollar had become less dominant in world economic affairs, and also because of the emergence of Japan and West Germany as powerful economic players. A system of general floating emerged at the beginning of 1973.

As will be discussed below, both fixed and floating rate systems have advantages and disadvantages. During the latc 1970s members of the European Community initiated the first steps on the way to full European monetary union. The European Monetary System (EMS) was aimed at the stabilisation of exchange rate movements between currencies, but without the extreme rigidity of the fixed exchange rate system which existed before 1971.

❑ Floating exchange rates

Under this system in its purest form, central banks make no attempt to influence movements in the exchange rate of their national currencies by direct intervention. The exchange rate finds its own level through the operation of the forces of supply and demand. In practice, however, no currency has floated completely freely. Central bank intervention has been frequent, and at times extensive, and has sometimes represented co-ordinated action between major central banks to prevent volatility, or to attempt to limit or resist market forces. Such intervention will only succeed in resisting market forces in the short run. At some point it becomes essential to deal with the economic fundamentals in order to achieve a permanent change in a currency's fortunes.

8.4 Floating and fixed: which is better?

There is a continuing debate on the merits of the two systems. The main arguments for and against each regime are shown below. It will be noted that some of the arguments can be used in two ways. For instance, some advantages of floating become disadvantages of fixed rates, but in the following section the argument appears only once.

❑ Advantages of floating exchange rates

Freely floating exchange rates provide an automatic adjustment to the balance of payments. For example, if a country is experiencing a current account deficit, the excess of imports over exports will drive down the exchange rate, making imports more expensive and exports cheaper to foreign buyers. The exchange rate will adjust until the demand for the currency (for current and capital account transactions) is in equilibrium with the supply (for current and capital account transactions), i.e. there is an overall balance of payments equilibrium.

Under a freely floating exchange rate regime, there is no need for large holdings of gold and foreign currencies, or for international borrowing to support the domestic currency.

Domestic policies can be pursued independently of constraints imposed by the need to keep the exchange rate at an agreed level.

❑ Disadvantages of floating exchange rates

Floating exchange rates introduce uncertainty into international transactions and destabilise trade.

A continuous fall in the exchange rate produces inflation because imported raw materials and other gooods become progressively more expensive.

If the elasticities of demand for a country's goods are unfavourable, the process of exchange rate adjustment may not work smoothly.

❑ Advantages of fixed exchange rates

They encourage international trade because of the elimination of a large element of foreign exchange risk. Longer-term planning is easier because revenue, costs and net returns can be calculated.

Fixed exchange rates impose a discipline on governments to pursue sound domestic policies, such as the control of inflation, to maintain the existing exchange rate.

❑ Disadvantages of fixed exchange rates

Differences in economic performance, particularly as regards inflation, make it impossible to retain a fixed exchange rate structure over time.

Speculation mounts when it becomes evident that a currency is over-valued or under-valued.

8.5 Trade-weighted (effective) rates

❑ The absence of a fixed reference point against which to measure changes in exchange rates has created difficulties in gauging the overall change in a country's currency against those of its main trading partners.

❑ Trade-weighted exchange rate indices have been established to resolve this, and are now widely used to measure one currency's performance against a combination of other currencies.

❑ In constructing an index, decisions need to be made regarding the country coverage, the base date and trading patterns. For example, the Bank of England index covers eighteen countries, uses 1985 as its base date and takes into consideration the importance of each country's trade with the other countries in the basket by utilising a weighting system. Thus each change from 100 in the index measures the movement of any particular currency against all other currencies in the basket from the base date, taking into consideration that country's trading pattern.

8.6 The European Monetary System (EMS)

❑ Background

Economic and Monetary Union (EMU) has become a major issue in the future development of the European Community, especially since the publication of the so-called Delors Report in 1989. An Inter-Governmental Conference to agree proposed amendments to the Treaty of Rome formally opened in December 1990 and culminated in a Summit in Maastricht in December 1991.

An important first step towards monetary union in the EC was the establishment of a system for stabilising movements bewteen currencies. The European Monetary System (EMS) was created in the late 1970s and formally started operating in March 1979 with this objective.

❑ Aims of the EMS

- To provide a zone of currency stability in Europe within the general floating exchange rate regime.
- To promote a convergence of economic policies in the EEC.
- To develop as a long-term goal European monetary union.

❑ Features of the EMS

In order to achieve the above aims, the following were introduced:

- A managed float to foster the continuing alignment of currencies at existing rates. This is the Exchange Rate Mechanism (ERM). Most EC countries are participants. The UK joined in October 1990 and Portugal in 1992.
- Short and medium-term finance is made available to countries which need to support the value of their currency. Each country placed 20% of its gold and dollar reserves in a central fund - the European Monetary Co-operation Fund (EMCF) - for this purpose.

❑ The ECU

EMS also involved the creation of a new currency, the European Currency Unit (ECU) to act as a unit of account in EC financial transactions. The ECU is a weighted basket of all EC currencies, the weight for each currency being based on individual countries' size in terms of GNP and the importance of their currency in EC trade. As a currency basket, it may be compared with the IMF's Special drawing rights (SDR).

The ECU serves four basic functions:

- the denominator for the exchange rate mechanism.
- the basis for the divergence indicator.
- the denominator for operations in both the intervention and credit mechanisms.
- a means of settlement between EMS members' central banks.

The attraction of the ECU as a basket currency (giving it in-built stability) has encouraged the gradual expansion of its private use and the emergence of an ECU money market. Many commercial banks now offer ECU-denominated deposit facilities and loans. There is also a ECU bond market.

❑Mechanics of the Exchange Rate Mechanism

Each currency has an ECU-related central rate. These rates are an integral part of the rules for exchange rate movements which are based on a 'grid' of bilateral exchange rates between members. Currencies generally are allowed to move up to 2.25% either side of the central rates , although in mid-1992 Spain, the UK and Portugal were still operating in a wider band of 6%. At the time of writing (Summer 1992) there were ten currencies in the ERM, with only the Greek drachma not participating in the system.

The system has a 'divergence indicator' which is triggered at 75% of the above movement and is an 'early warning' that currencies are getting out of line. Governments must then take the necessary steps to adjust their economic policies and may draw on certain credit facilities which are available to support exchange rates.

EMS EUROPEAN CURRENCY UNIT RATES (as at 6 July 1992)

1	2	3	4	5	6
Escudo	178.74	171.10	- 4.27	6.12	70
Peseta	133.63	129.39	- 3.18	4.92	54
Belgian Franc	42.40	42.15	- 0.60	2.20	29
DeutscheMark	2.06	2.05	- 0.40	2.00	26
Guilder	2.32	2.31	- 0.36	1.96	18
French Franc	6.89	6.90	+ 0.03	1.56	- 2
Irish Punt	0.77	0.77	+ 0.05	1.54	- 2
Danish Krone	7.84	7.87	+ 0.37	1.22	- 17
Lira	1,538.24	1,549.24	+ 0.74	0.84	- 37
Sterling	0.70	0.71	+ 1.59	0.00	- 32

Key to columns

1 currency
2 ECU central rates (rounded up)
3 currency amounts against ECU
4 percentage change against central rate
5 percentage spread against weakest currency
6 divergence indicator

❑ Economic and Monetary Union in Europe

The ultimate aim of EMU is for the EC to have a single currency, common monetary policy and a European Central Bank. The Maastricht Summit proposed implementation from 1 January 1999. Politics, however, intervened, and politics, rather than economics will dominate the debate over the coming years. With individual economies in Europe still divergent in terms of inflation rates, government borrowing, institutional structures etc., member states have agreed that movement to a single currency should not take place until the economic performance of the participating countries has converged to a satisfactory degree.

The convergence criteria embodied in the treaty cover four key areas:

1. Inflation must be within 1.5 percentage points of the average of the three best performing member states for a period of one year.

2. Fiscal discipline is conditional on government deficits not exceeding 3% of GDP and stock of government debt not exceeding 60% of GDP.
3. The participating countries are required to have demonstrated their ability to survive in a fixed exchange rate environment by observing the narrow margins of the ERM without initiating a realignment for a period of at least two years.
4. Long-term inflation rates must be within 2 percentage points of the best performing member states in terms of price stability for a period of one year.

8.7 Exchange rates and interest rates

There is a close relationship between exchange rates and interest rates. Governments can raise interest rates in order to attract short-term investment, thereby strengthening the exchange rate. A fall in interest rates makes the currency less attractive to hold and the exchange rate is likely to fall.

The above, of course, assumes that interest rates are the *only* factor influencing exchange rates. In fact raising interest rates will never be enough to 'defend' a currency if other factors, e.g. high inflation, large balance of payments deficits, political unrest, are seen to be more important. Likewise, cutting interest rates will only deter foreign investors if they are convinced that the currency is either not going to rise in value anyway or that there is an alternative currency (or gold) to invest in safetly. The Swiss government has at times imposed negative interest rates on foreign holders of Swiss francs in order to prevent the exchange rate from rising.

There is therefore no really *quantifiable* direct relationship between *spot* exchange rates and interest rates. However, there is a more real link between *forward* exchange rates and interest rates:

- The currency with the higher interest rate will sell at a *discount* in the forward exchange market against the currency with a lower interest rate.

- The currency with the lower interest rate will sell at a *premium* in the forward market against the currency with the higher interest rate.

The forward premium or discount brings interest rates into a relationship whereby an investment in any convertible currency would result in the same return or cost as an investment in any other currency, since the annualised discount or premium equals the interest rate differential (see Unit 5.5).

questions and answers

Q 1 (a) For what reasons might a country's central bank intervene in the foreign exchange markets?
(b) To what extent is intervention by a country's central bank likely to succeed in affecting the exchange rate of that country's currency?

(Autumn 1986)

Answer

(a) (i) To keep a currency's exchange rate within agreed limits (e.g. EMS).
(ii) To prevent sharp fluctuations in the rate
(iii) To devalue the rate to boost exports
(iv) To revalue the rate to curb inflation

(b) In the short term intervention can help, but to effect a long-term change, action is required on the fundamentals.

Q 2 (a) What factors determine long-term movements in a country's exchange rate? (9)
(b) Discuss the case for and against a return to a worldwide system of fixed exchange rates. (16)

(Spring 1987)

Answer

(a) See section 8.2
(b) See section 8.4.

Q 3 (a) To what extent does the theory of purchasing power parity explain a change in a country's exchange rate? (13)
(b) Examine the consequences of a depreciating exchange rate on a country's
 (i) current account of the balance of payments (9)
 (ii) inflation rate (3)

(Autumn 1988)

Answer
(a) The theory explains long-term movements - see section 8.2
(b) (i) See section 7.4
 (ii) Imports will cost more - pushing up the inflation rate

Q 4 (a) Outline the main objectives of the European Monetary System (EMS). (5)
(b) What economic conditions are essential for the objectives of EMS to be achieved? (8)

(Spring 1989)

Answer
(a) See section 8.6
(b) Convergence of economic policies - in particular bring inflation to approximately common levels; reduce interest rate differentials; eliminate persistently large balance of payments differences on current account

Q 5 (a) Outline the reasons which might lead a central bank to intervene on the foreign exchange markets. (11)
(b) Apart from imposing exchange controls, how might a central bank intervene to influence the exchange rate? (6)
(c) Can central bank intervention succeed in stabilising a country's exchange rate in the long term? Give reasons for your answer. (8)

(Autumn 1989)

Answer
(a) See Q1 above
(b) Direct intervention - purchases/sales of foreign currencies
Indirect intervention - interest rates or economic policy generally
(c) No - the economic fundamentals (see Section 8.2) have to be addressed.

Unit Nine
Supervision and Regulation

9.1 The role of the Bank of England

The Bank of England's responsibilities for controlling banking activities in the UK were formulated under the 1979 and 1987 Banking Acts. Prior to the 1979 Act, the supervision of banks was conducted largely on an informal basis.

The Acts taken together provide for the first time a comprehensive framework for the control by the Bank of England of banking operations in the UK, with the aims of:

- protecting depositors against loss;
- maintaining the general health and stability of the financial system.

The Banking Act 1987 replaced the 1979 Act as the statutory basis for banking supervision. The main provisions were:

❑ A *Board of Banking Supervision* was established within the Bank of England to help the Governor in supervising the banking system;

❑ deposit-taking institutions must obtain authorisation from the Bank of England, which sets minimum prudential requirements, eg for capital and liquidity (see below - Prudential Controls);

❑ authorised institutions must maintain suitable accounting and other records, and internal control systems, all of which are monitored by the Bank;

❑ banks are required to advise the Bank of England of any large exposure (over 10% of capital) to a single customer, and prior notice must be given of proposed transactions which exceed 25% of capital;

❑ the *Deposit Protection Scheme*, established under the 1979 Act, was extended. The scheme offers insurance to ordinary depositors of 75% of the first £20,000 of sterling deposits made with an institution's UK offices.

❑ Prudential Controls

These form part of the Bank of England's duties to ensure the stability and health of the banking system. Four basic areas are addressed:

- capital adequacy
- liquidity
- foreign currency exposure
- risk

Capital adequacy requirements involve both the definition of what constitutes capital and how much each bank should have. With banks having to compete internationally, it is desirable that capital requirements are standardised around the world, to achieve a 'level playing field'. In recent years, attempts have been made to bring about such standardisation or 'convergence' of capital adequacy under the aegis of the Committee on Banking Regulations and Supervisory Practices of the Bank for International Settlements (BIS). This agreement (the Basle Accord) covers the large majority of the world's leading banks.

The key features of the agreement are:

- capital equivalent to at least 8% of assets weighted according to risk must be maintained;
- at least half the capital base must consist of equity and disclosed reserves (Tier 1 capital);
- remaining capital consists of items such as revaluation reserves, general provisions, hidden reserves and subordinated debt (Tier 2 capital);
- in calculating the capital requirement, off-balance sheet items will be taken into account by using conversion factors to establish their credit risk equivalent;
- each country may apply its own criteria, using the accord as a minimum.

Liquidity is required for the reasons outlined in section 2.3. The Bank of England has set out liquidity requirements to ensure that banks meet their obligations. Banks must:

- hold sufficient cash or liquid assets;
- secure an appropriately matching future profile of cash flows from maturing assets;
- maintain an adequately diversified deposit base.

Responsibility for ensuring the liquidity of a particular bank rests with its own management. The Bank does not seek to impose across-the-board liquidity ratio norms. The Bank sees its supervisory role as ensuring that a bank applies a prudent mix of different forms of liquidity appropriate to the circumstances of each particular bank, and that these policies are sustained at all times.

Foreign currency exposure: the Bank seeks to measure, monitor and discuss with banks their exposure to movements in exchange rates. The Bank monitors banks' net currency positions - the difference between assets and liabilities in individual currencies - and sets guidelines for such positions both in individual currencies and in total net positions in all currencies.

Risk supervision involves monitoring large exposures and the degree of risk attaching to individual assets. Some assets, such as Treasury bills require little or no capital cover, others require to be highly covered by capital.

9.2 European Community (EC) regulations

The EC has, under various Banking Directives, established formal requirements for bank authorisation, supervision, large exposures and capital adequacy. These requirements, which are closely related to those laid down under the UK's 1987 Banking Act and the BIS capital adequacy provision (see Section 9.1), establish a 'level playing field' for banks operating in the Community.

The next stage, which forms an integral part of the completion of the Single European Market by 1992, involves the removal of obstacles to the provision of banking services by individual institutions Europe-wide.

The *Second Banking Co-ordination Directive* would entitle a financial institution such as a bank or building society to market a wide range of services throughout the Community, without the need to obtain further authorisation in other member states.

The European Community is now seeking to produce legislation which will lay down common financial conditions for banks and securities houses in their investment business.

9.3 The Third World debt problem and the banks

The problem of lesser developed countries (LDC) debt began in the 1970s as commercial banks arranged large loans with few strings attached for many developing countries with current account deficits. The ease with which such loans could be arranged, and the eagerness of banks to lend, meant that such countries could continue to run current account deficits throughout the 1970s and early 1980s in the knowledge that capital inflows would be forthcoming to finance such deficits.

The idea that lending to sovereign countries was inherently safe began to be questioned as the debt-servicing obligations of the borrowers exceeded 30%, 40% or even 60% of their foreign exchange receipts. Banks became less eager to lend further money, and LDCs began to experience difficulties in covering their external obligations. In 1982, the difficulties of servicing huge foreign debts became manifestly too onerous. Mexico declared a moratorium on debt repayments, and began negotiations with creditors on rescheduling payments. Many other highly indebted countries followed suit. For the rest of the 1980s, economic retrenchment - involving slow growth (often below the pace of population increase) - has been necessary to reduce or eliminate chronic current account deficits. However, the surpluses required actually to repay debt are beyond the capacity of the countries concerned. The result has been a loss to commercial banks in terms of:

- depletion of profits as provisions for possible defaults have had to be made;

- reduction in the value of assets as debt is sold at well below face value in the secondary market, where discounts can be 90% or even more;
- because profits have been depleted, the banks' shareholders' funds and thus capital has been correspondingly depressed.

9.4 Regulation and supervision of investment business

The regulation of investment business in the UK is covered by the *Financial Services Act 1986*. Under this Act, the Department of Trade and Industry is responsible for overall regulation of the industry, with operational powers delegated to the Securities and Investments Board (SIB).

❑ The act aims to protect investors' interests by ensuring that investment business is carried out only by firms and individuals considered 'fit and proper', and duly authorised by the SIB to carry out such business;

❑ Criteria for authorisation are: capital adequacy; good business record; good character of managers, directors; compliance arrangements; business operations plan;

❑ It is a criminal offence for any person to operate an investment business without prior authorisation;

❑ In order to keep their authorisation, firms must comply with the rules and codes of conduct laid down by the SIB and its satellites - five self-regulatory organisations (SROs) established to supervise firms in their specialist areas - such as life assurance and unit trusts, securities, investment management.

❑ The rules/codes of conduct with which investment firms must comply are: businesses must operate with integrity and act fairly; they must practice due skill and diligence; they must adopt high standards of market conduct; they must avoid conflicts of interest; assets of investors must be separate from business assets; adequate resources must be maintained; internal administration must be closely monitored.

❑ While the SIB system is responsible for specific investment activities, the Act gives the Bank of England responsibility for the regulation of markets - gilts, bullion, wholesale money and foreign exchange.

❑ A compensation fund was set up, funded by authorised businesses. The fund provides compensation to investors for the first £30,000 of individual investments and 90% cover for the next £20,000 in the event of loss due to the insolvency or fraud of an authorised firm.

9.5 Regulation and supervision of building societies

Building societies under the Building Societies Act 1986 are the responsibility of the Building Societies Commission, which is accountable to the Treasury. The Commission is required to:

- promote the financial stability of building societies;
- promote the protection of shareholders'/depositors' funds;
- promote building society aims, notably the making of loans for house purchase.

As with the Bank of England and the SIB, the Commission is required to attend to the authorisation of institutions for which it has responsibility. The criteria for authorisation are similar to those imposed by the Bank of England, in that they relate to:

- capital and liquidity adequacy;
- suitable accounting records and internal systems;
- the quality of directors and officers.

9.6 Regulation and supervision of insurance companies

The Department of Trade and Industry (DTI) is responsible for implementing the provisions of the Insurance Companies Act 1982 which has two main aims:

- to protect policy holders from the failure of an insurance company
- to protect individuals from being sold policies unsuited to their needs.

The DTI has the following powers to carry out its responsibilities effectively:

- authorisation of insurance businesses
- laying down capital requirements
- monitoring businesses
- intervention if necessary in running businesses

The 1982 Act makes it a criminal offence for an individual or company to carry out insurance business without DTI authorisation, which is given only to 'fit and proper' applicants.

questions and answers

Q1 Outline the ways in which the Bank of England

(a) supervises and regulates the activities of the banks in the UK; (17)

(b) ensures that there is always adequate liquidity in the banking system. (8)

(Spring 1991)

Answer

(a) See section 9.1, focusing on capital adequacy, liquidity, currency exposure and risk supervision.

(b) See section 3.1.

Q2 (a) (i) For what reasons does a commercial bank need liquidity? (8)

(ii) How may liquidity be provided? (11)

(b) How does the Bank of England currently exercise its supervisory role with regard to commercial banks' liquidity? (6)

(Autumn 1991)

Answer

(a) See section 2.3

(b) See section 9.1

Q3 (a) Outline the areas of responsibility of the main bodies involved in supervising and regulating investment business in the UK. (18)

(b) What protection do these bodies offer investors against losses on their investments? (7)

(Spring 1992)

Answer

(a) See section 9.4

(b) See section 9.4

Unit Ten
Corporate Finance and Risk Management

Financial institutions exist to service their customers. For exclusively 'retail' banks and, of course, building societies, these are mostly private individuals. The corporate sector, however, representing small, medium and large (including public, limited) companies is a major user of financial services. Companies are a source of deposits for banks but, more importantly, are significant borrowers. Corporates, as opposed to individuals, also make greater use of the more 'sophisticated' financial products to limit (hedge) risks associated with fluctuations in exchange rates and interest rates. This chapter briefly describes the ways in which companies raise finance and concludes with a section on hedging.

10.1 Short-term finance

Bank overdrafts are still the most common form of funding by companies. It is a very flexible method of borrowing ideally suited to day-to-day financing needs: easy to arrange with the minimum of documentation. In theory, overdrafts are repayable on demand and the rate charged is usually a margin above the bank's base rate on the residual amount.

Money market loans represent borrowing by companies at 'wholesale' rather than retail interest rates. Market 'lines' are fixed in term and amount and may be denominated in any currency. The reference rate is usually LIBOR (London Interbank Offered Rate) and drawings can be as short as overnight, but are normally at one, three or six months with the loan being 'rolled over' at each maturity. The actual interest rate will be re-fixed at the rollover date. Market lines often involve a commitment fee payable to the bank at the time of drawdown, usually related to the undrawn element of the facility.

Acceptance credits are a traditional form of short-term finance whereby a company draws a bill of exchange on a bank. If the bank 'accepts' the bill it is, in effect, guaranteeing payment at maturity, for a fee. Bills of Exchange which have been accepted by an 'eligible' bank are eligible for re-discount at the Bank of England.

Companies commonly set up acceptance facilities with their bankers which automatically allow them to draw bills up to a specified amount. The finance is provided by the bank on-selling the accepted bill in the bill market and passing the discounted proceeds to the customer (who will then reimburse the bank for the face amount of the bill on maturity). Acceptance commission (the fee) is charged by the bank and the rate at which the bills are discounted reflects current rates prevailing in the money markets.

Commercial paper (CP) represents a short-term promissory note issued by medium and large public limited companies of good standing. CP is an alternative source of funds to the more traditional bank loans or bills, and is an example of disintermediation. The advantage of CP is that it is a relatively cheap and flexible form of borrowing. In contrast to commercial bills, CP does not have to be issued as a counterpart to a specific transaction. Maturities normally range from seven days up to one year. CP is issued at a discount to face value and the discount rate is usually linked to LIBID. Apart from sterling commercial paper, US dollar paper and euro-commercial paper are also actively traded in the London money markets.

10.2 Medium/long-term finance

It is usual to distinguish between short-term (under one year), medium-term (one to five years) and long-term finance (over five years), although this is little more than a matter of convenience. Borrowers and investors both wish to spread their risks along the yield curve and various financial products have evolved to meet their different needs. The most significant development, however, in recent years has been the swaps market (discussed later) which has effectively blurred the distinction between shorter and longer-term finance. Bank loans for periods in excess of twenty-five years are no longer a rare occurrence, particularly when swaps also form part of the transaction. The banks' involvement in the personal home mortgage market is extensive - even though they did not become major lenders until the 1980s.

Medium-term notes (MTNs)

The market in sterling MTNs was opened in February 1990. MTNs are very similar to commercial paper apart from the maturity range which goes from usually one year to five years, and even ten years. MTNs can be issued in a variety of currencies. The cost of issuing MTNs for corporates includes underwriting and arrangement fees, with the interest cost based on LIBID. MTNs have grown in popularity with corporate treasurers because they are very flexible and the costs of issue are low.

Bonds

Companies issue loan stock (often referred to as bonds or debentures) usually to fund specific long-term projects. Interest is usually fixed at the outset and maturities can range from five to twenty-five years. Bonds are attractive as a method of funding because interest is tax-deductible (as an expense of the business) unlike dividends on ordinary shares which are paid out of post-tax income. Bonds can also be issued with an option to convert (ie 'convertibles') into ordinary shares or equity.

Eurobonds

Eurobonds are securities denominated in currency (ie offshore) and are used by large multinational corporations to raise significant amounts. Eurobonds are often 'rated' by credit agencies, such as Moody's and Standard and Poor's. Eurobonds are fixed-term but may be issued with either a fixed or floating rate of interest. Eurobonds can be issued as convertibles or with 'warrants' attached, which give the bondholder a right to purchase ordinary shares in the issuing company at a pre-determined price.

Eurobonds are useful for corporate treasurers because they can be issued in a variety of currencies (eg to match the currency and income stream of the project being financed) and therefore at different interest rates. The

Eurobond market is also much less regulated in terms of documentation, legal requirements and tax, etc which can often make it easier for companies to raise funds offshore compared with their own domestic markets.

10.3 Equity finance

The existence of shares and shareholders is an important feature of market economics. Shares represent permanent capital and pay dividends rather than interest. Ordinary shareholders own a part of the company in which they invest and share capital is that which is left over when all the claims against a company have been met, ie equity. By definition ordinary shares are the most risky investments in a company and, therefore, have the greatest potential for profit.

For a company, ordinary shares have the advantage of permanence and, in the event of the company suffering a serious downturn in its trading performance, the dividend can be lowered or even waived completely. Preference shares offer fixed dividend payments but usually have no voting rights.

The significance of equity in the financial structure of a company is its long-term nature and all corporations need to achieve a balance between their short-term and long-term financing needs. A larger element of debt, as opposed to equity, could cause difficulties for a company if interest rates rise sharply and this was seen most clearly in the 'junk bond' crisis in the US at the end of the 1980s. The relationship between equity and debt is often referred to as the capital gearing ratio.

10.4 Rate Risk Management

All companies have to deal with the issue of fluctuating interest rates and multinational companies have the additional problem of volatile movements in foreign exchange rates. Rate risk management describes what these risks are and the ways in which company treasurers may reduce or 'hedge' against them.

❑ Interest rate risk

Companies are 'exposed' to movements in interest rates, whether they go up or down. Either as borrowers or investors (depositors), corporate treasurers essentially have a choice between fixed or variable (floating) interest rates. Private individuals are faced with the same choices, ie if they are borrowers, do they use overdrafts knowing that the interest cost can change any day or do they take a fixed rate personal loan? If they are saving money, do they leave it on an account which provides easy access and a fluctuating rate of interest or do they invest for a fixed term (probably at a higher rate)? Whether interest rates rise or fall, someone (corporation or individual) will benefit and someone will lose.

Hedging attempts to minimise the negative impact of interest rate movements for both borrowers and investors and some hedging products, notably options, provide the *possibility* of gain whatever happens to interest rates.

❑ Hedging techniques

There are a number of hedges against interest rate risk, including financial futures and interest rate options. However, the main techniques are:

Interest rate swaps

Interest rate swaps allow companies to exchange their interest rate obligations with one another, usually through a financial intermediary such as a bank.

Swaps exist because some companies are able to raise long-term fixed rate funds more cheaply than others. However, they may prefer to have repayments based on floating rates and can do so by swapping their fixed rate commitments with another counterparty. The most important aspect of interest rate swap transactions is that companies exchange interest payments, but not the nominal amounts underlying the transactions.

Swaps allow companies to exchange fixed rate obligations for floating rate obligations and will reflect companies' different perceptions of future interest rate movements. Companies can also swap interest rate obligations in different currencies, although where such 'currency swaps' are concerned, there is an actual exchange of principal involved.

Forward Rate Agreements (FRAs)
Borrowers are concerned that interest rates may rise in the future, thus increasing the company's cost of funding. Investors are concerned with the opposite, ie that interest rates will fall and the return will be less than desired. FRAs provide a means by which the interest rate can be fixed in advance for a specific period of time. For example, a company borrowing at floating rate and expecting interest rates to rise may enter into an FRA with a bank, fixing the *future* rate at a specific level, say 14%, for a specific period, either three or six months.

If rates rise above 14%, the bank will pay the borrower the difference between 14% and the actual (higher) cost of borrowing. If rates fall below 14% the borrower will pay the bank the difference. In this way a company can hedge against rates rising beyond a certain level but, of course, foregoes the benefit of interest rates falling. This essentially is the cost of the hedge. Futures can also be used to hedge interest rate exposure, and there are other 'derivatives' such as 'caps' and 'collars' which effectively fix future interest rates, or at least limit the movement in rates.

10.5 Exchange Rate Risk

Companies are exposed to movements in exchange rates whether they are importers or exporters *(transaction exposure)* and when they own assets or have liabilities in different currencies from that of their 'home' balance sheet *(translation exposure)*. There are many ways to hedge exchange rate risk, from the simple pooling or 'netting' of currency liabilities and assets, to very complex structures using swaps and options, etc. Two major techniques are described on the next page.

Forward exchange contracts
When a company is expecting either to receive or to pay out foreign currency in the future, it can enter into a forward contract with a bank. The bank contracts with the customer to sell or purchase a fixed amount of currency at a future date at a rate of exchange fixed at the date of the contract. Usually the future date is specified but 'option forwards' give the customer the flexibility to close out the contract on a variety of dates. Forward contracts involve the physical delivery of the currency purchased or sold (by the bank or the customer) and the contract must be honoured. As mentioned in Unit Five there is a cost

involved which is represented by the premium or discount at which the forward currency stands in relation to the spot exchange rate.

Currency options

Currency options give the *purchaser* the right but not the obligation to buy or sell (call or put) a specified amount of currency at an agreed rate at a date in the future. For European options the date is fixed, whilst American options can be exercised any time up to the expiry date. The important difference from forward exchange contracts is that the customer does not have to exercise the option. In other words, if exchange rates do not move adversely and in fact move in the customer's favour, then the option can be lapsed, or even sold to another counterparty.

The premium paid for a currency option can be likened to an insurance premium (most people do not expect to claim!) and options generally are more expensive than plain forward contracts. However, they are more flexible and provide the possibility for making a profit from the option as well as giving the desired protection ('hedge') against adverse movements in exchange rates.

questions and answers

Q1 The Finance Director of a small manufacturing company is concerned about the financial risks the company faces as it expands its business at home and abroad. He approaches you for advice. Explain to him:

(a) the main interest and exchange rate risks facing a company (9)

(b) how a company can protect itself against the risks you have discussed in (a). (16)

(Spring 1991)

Answer: *(a) See sections 10.4 and 10.5*

Q2 The finance director of a large manufacturing business informs you that his company is likely to require short-term finance.

(a) Outline the main methods available to the company to meet its short-term financing requirements. (13)

(b) Discuss the advantages to the company of any THREE of the methods you have identified in (a). (12)

(Autumn 1991)

Answer: *See section 10.1*

index

Acceptance credits	99
Aggregates (money)	3
Balance of payments:	69-77
capital account	72-73
current account	71-72
deficits	73-77
exchange rates	76
import control	76
terms of trade	71
Bank balance sheets	14-15
Bank of England:	
functions	18-21
role	25-26
supervision	91-93
Banking Act 1987	91-92
'Broad' money	2
Building Societies	20-21
supervision	96
CD market	28
Capital adequacy	92
Capital markets	33-34
Commercial paper	29,99
Corporate finance	98
Credit creation	37-39
Currency swaps	104
Disintermediation	11
EC banking regulations	93-94
ECU	86
EMS	85-88
EMU	88
ERM	86-87
Economic Policy	
aims	58-59
exchange rate policy	65-66
fiscal policy	64-65
monetary policy	59-64
prices and income policy	65
Equity finance	101
Eurobonds	32,100
Eurocurrency markets:	31-33
controls	32-33
interest rates	54-56
Exchange rates:	79-89
adjustments	76-77
interest rates	88-89
movements	80-81
policy	65-66
swaps	102
systems	81-84
trade-weighted rates	84
Finance houses	22
Finance house market	29
Financial intermediation	10
Financial Services Act 1986	95
Fiscal policy	64-65
Foreign banks	16
Forward Rate Agreements	103
Futures (LIFFE) market	29-30
GEMMS	16,34
Gold	74
Hedging	102-3
IMF	74-75
Index-linking	6
Inflation	5,6,44 49,75
Insurance companies	22, 96-97
Inter-bank market	28
Interest rates:	47-56
changes	52-53
exchange rates	54-56
real & nominal rates	47-48
yield curve	51
Investment trusts	22

LIFFE 29-30
Liquidity (bank) 16-18
Local Authority market 28
London Discount Market 27-28

MO-M5 3
M4 42-4
Medium term notes 29,100
Merchant banks 16
Monetary policy: 59-64
Money:
aggregates 3
functions 1
liquidity 1-2
narrow and broad money 2
quantity theory 4-5
targets 4
Money market loans 98
Money supply 37-44
changes in 44
control of 44
credit creation 37-39
funding/overfunding 41
PSBR/PSDR 39-44
Multi-function facilities 99

Narrow money 2
National Savings Bank 21-22
Near-money 1

Open-market operations 62
Overdrafts 98
Overfunding 41

PSBR 39-44
PSDR 41
Pension funds 22
Parallel money markets 30

Quantity theory of money 4-5

REPOS 26
Regulation
banks 91-94
building societies 96
insurance companies 96-97
investment business 95-96

Retail banks 13
Retail price index (RPI) 7
Risk management 102-4
Round-tripping 50

SDRs 74
SEMBS 26,34
SIB 95
Swaps 32,102-3, 104

Third World debt problem 94-95

Unit Trusts 23

Yield curve 51-52